BASED ON THE *NEW YORK TIMES* BESTSELLING SERIES

Five Nights at Freddy's™

FAZBEAR FRIGHTS

GRAPHIC NOVEL COLLECTION VOL. 1

BY SCOTT CAWTHON,

ELLEY COOPER, AND CARLY ANNE WEST

ADAPTED BY CHRISTOPHER HASTINGS

INTO THE PIT

ILLUSTRATED BY DIDI ESMERALDA

COLORS BY EVA DE LA CRUZ

TO BE BEAUTIFUL

ILLUSTRATED BY ANTHONY MORRIS JR.

COLORS BY BEN SAWYER

OUT OF STOCK

ILLUSTRATED BY ANDI SANTAGATA

COLORS BY GONZALO DUARTE

LETTERS BY MICAH MYERS

ISBN 978-93-5471-897-7

This reprint edition, July 2025

Edited by Michael Petranek

Book design by Jeff Shake

Inks by Didi Esmeralda, Anthony Morris Jr., and Andi Santagata

Cover art: Emese Szigetvári

Colors by Eva De La Cruz, Ben Sawyer, and Gonzalo Duarte

Letters by Micah Myers

Printed in India: VK Global Digital Private Limited

INTO THE PIT

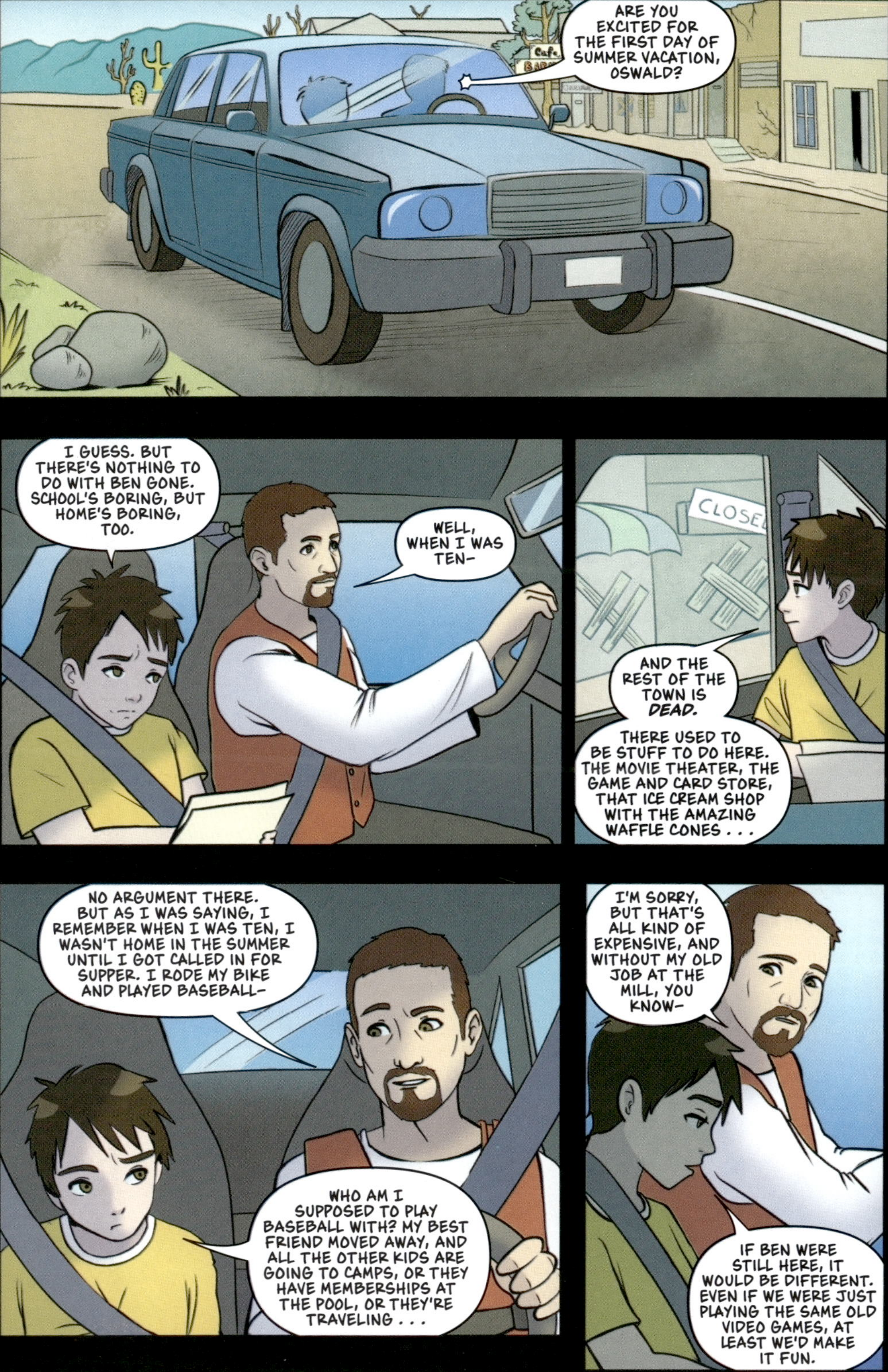

ARE YOU EXCITED FOR THE FIRST DAY OF SUMMER VACATION, OSWALD?

CLOSED

I GUESS. BUT THERE'S NOTHING TO DO WITH BEN GONE. SCHOOL'S BORING, BUT HOME'S BORING, TOO.

WELL, WHEN I WAS TEN-

AND THE REST OF THE TOWN IS *DEAD.*

THERE USED TO BE STUFF TO DO HERE. THE MOVIE THEATER, THE GAME AND CARD STORE, THAT ICE CREAM SHOP WITH THE AMAZING WAFFLE CONES . . .

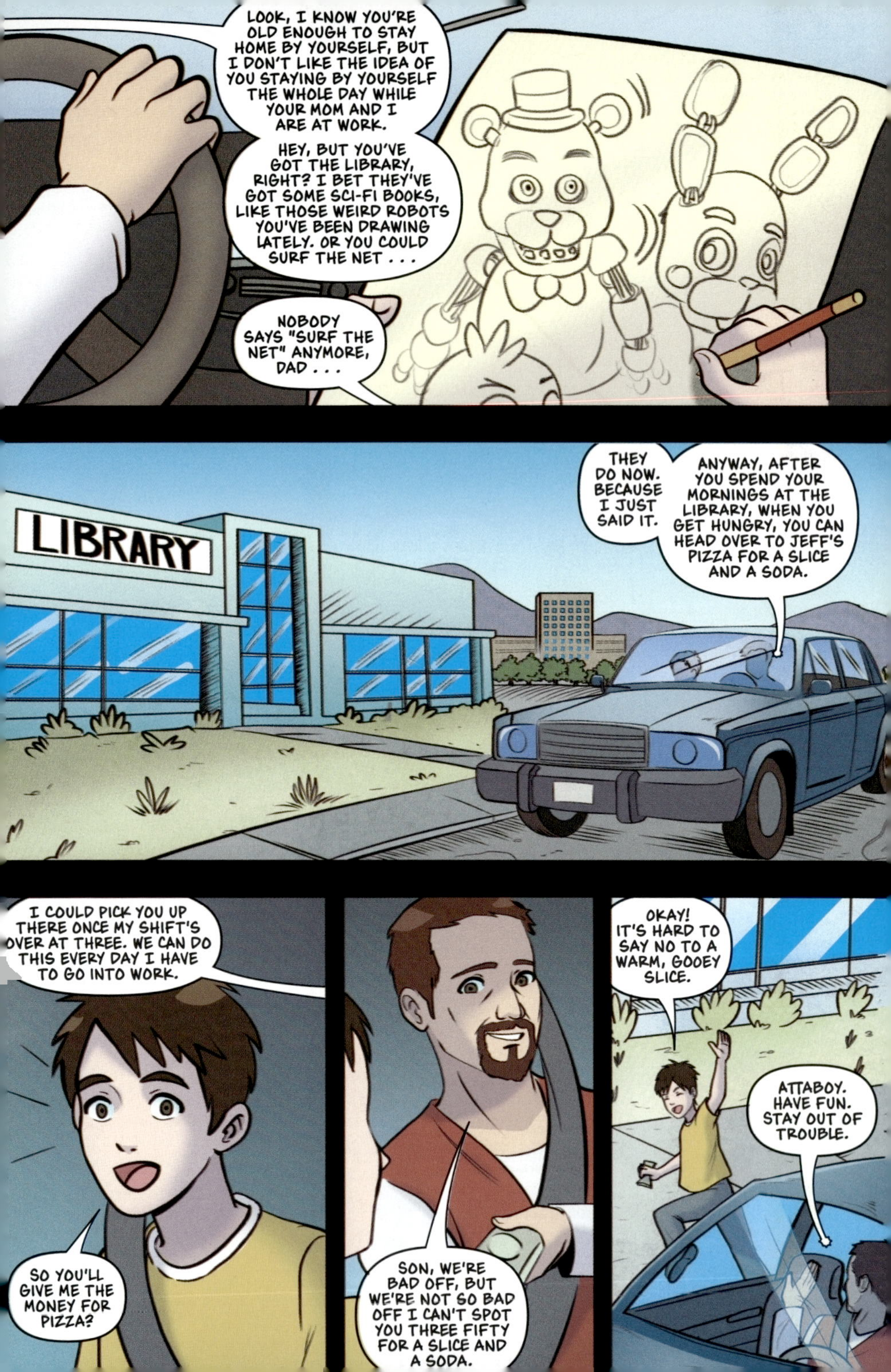

LOOK, I KNOW YOU'RE OLD ENOUGH TO STAY HOME BY YOURSELF, BUT I DON'T LIKE THE IDEA OF YOU STAYING BY YOURSELF THE WHOLE DAY WHILE YOUR MOM AND I ARE AT WORK.
HEY, BUT YOU'VE GOT THE LIBRARY, RIGHT? I BET THEY'VE GOT SOME SCI-FI BOOKS, LIKE THOSE WEIRD ROBOTS YOU'VE BEEN DRAWING LATELY. OR YOU COULD SURF THE NET . . .
NOBODY SAYS "SURF THE NET" ANYMORE, DAD . . .
LIBRARY
THEY DO NOW. BECAUSE I JUST SAID IT.
ANYWAY, AFTER YOU SPEND YOUR MORNINGS AT THE LIBRARY, WHEN YOU GET HUNGRY, YOU CAN HEAD OVER TO JEFF'S PIZZA FOR A SLICE AND A SODA.
I COULD PICK YOU UP THERE ONCE MY SHIFT'S OVER AT THREE. WE CAN DO THIS EVERY DAY I HAVE TO GO INTO WORK.
SO YOU'LL GIVE ME THE MONEY FOR PIZZA?
SON, WE'RE BAD OFF, BUT WE'RE NOT SO BAD OFF I CAN'T SPOT YOU THREE FIFTY FOR A SLICE AND A SODA.
OKAY! IT'S HARD TO SAY NO TO A WARM, GOOEY SLICE.
ATTABOY. HAVE FUN. STAY OUT OF TROUBLE.

LITERATURE
MATHEMATICS

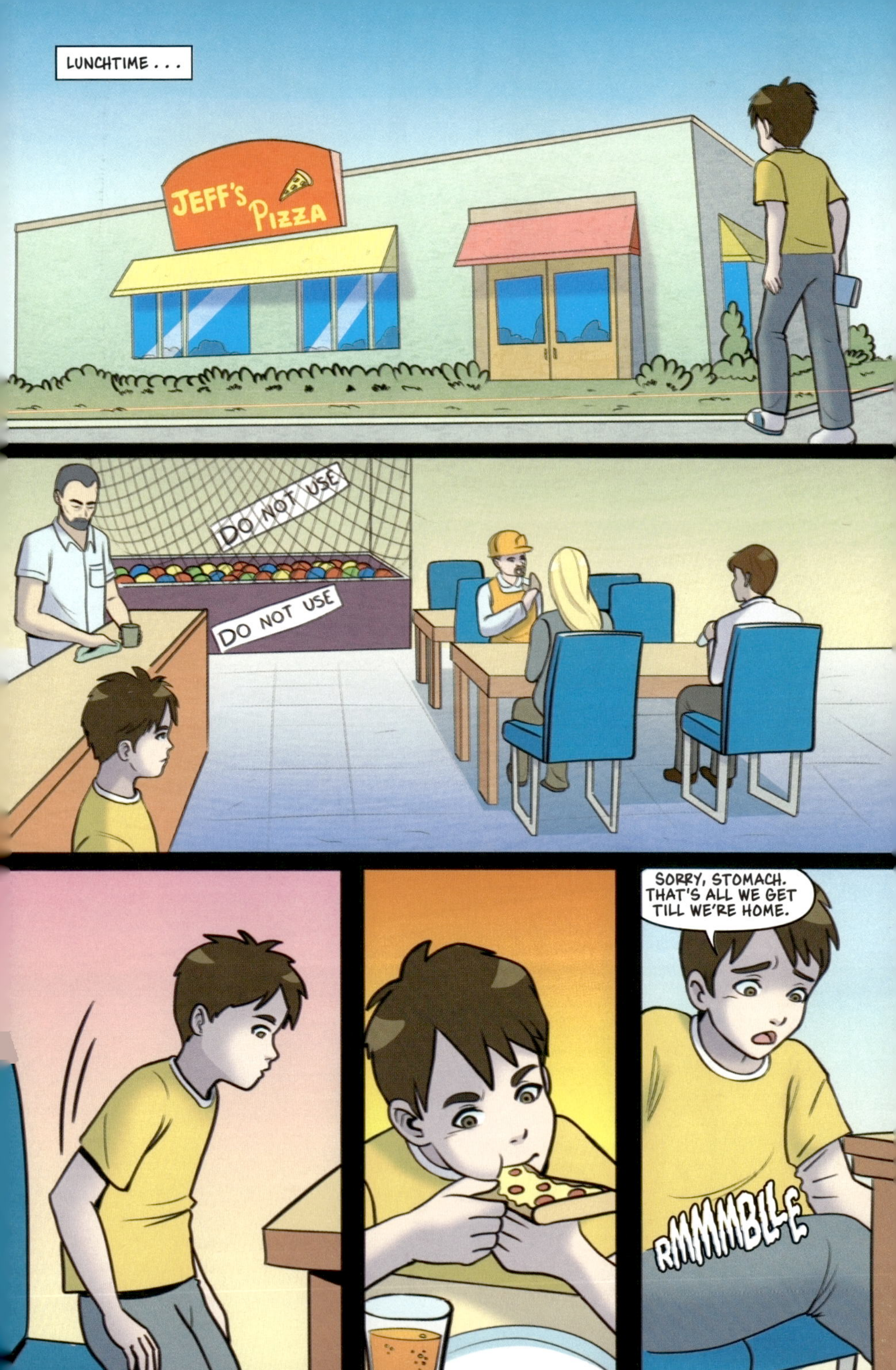
LUNCHTIME . . .
JEFF'S PIZZA
DO NOT USE
DO NOT USE
SORRY, STOMACH. THAT'S ALL WE GET TILL WE'RE HOME.
RMMMBLLE

DO NOT
DO NOT USE
KID.
AH! YES, SIR?
I GOT A COUPLE MORE CHEESE SLICES THAT DIDN'T SELL AT LUNCH. YOU WANT 'EM? ON THE HOUSE. I'D HAVE TO THROW 'EM OUT ANYWAY.

I'LL GET YOU SOME MORE ORANGE SODA WHILE I'M AT IT.
OH, OKAY. SURE. THANKS!
DAD:
Off work. Will be out front at jeff's in 2 min.
JEFF'S PIZZA
MAYBE THIS SUMMER MIGHT NOT BE SO BAD AFTER ALL . . .

LATER THAT EVENING . . .
WHO DO YOU THINK IS GOING TO WIN THIS ONE? ZENDRELIX OR MECHAZENDRELIX?
YOU KNOW I ALWAYS ROOT FOR ZENDRELIX.
WHAT? ZENDRELIX IS THE BAD GUY! THE MONSTER!
HE'S MEANT TO TERRIFY YOU!
COME ON, DAD, YOU CAN SEE THE ZIPPER! IT'S SOME ACTOR IN A RUBBER SUIT!
HOW SCARY COULD A GUY IN A SUIT BE?

LATER . . .
A PRETTY GOOD DAY . . .
I MIGHT NOT HAVE BEN.
AND I DON'T HAVE MONEY.
BUT I HAVE MONSTER MOVIES, AND THE LIBRARY, AND LUNCHTIME PIZZA SLICES.
. . .
WILL IT KEEP ME GOING ALL SUMMER, THOUGH?
PLEASE.
PLEASE LET SOMETHING INTERESTING HAPPEN.

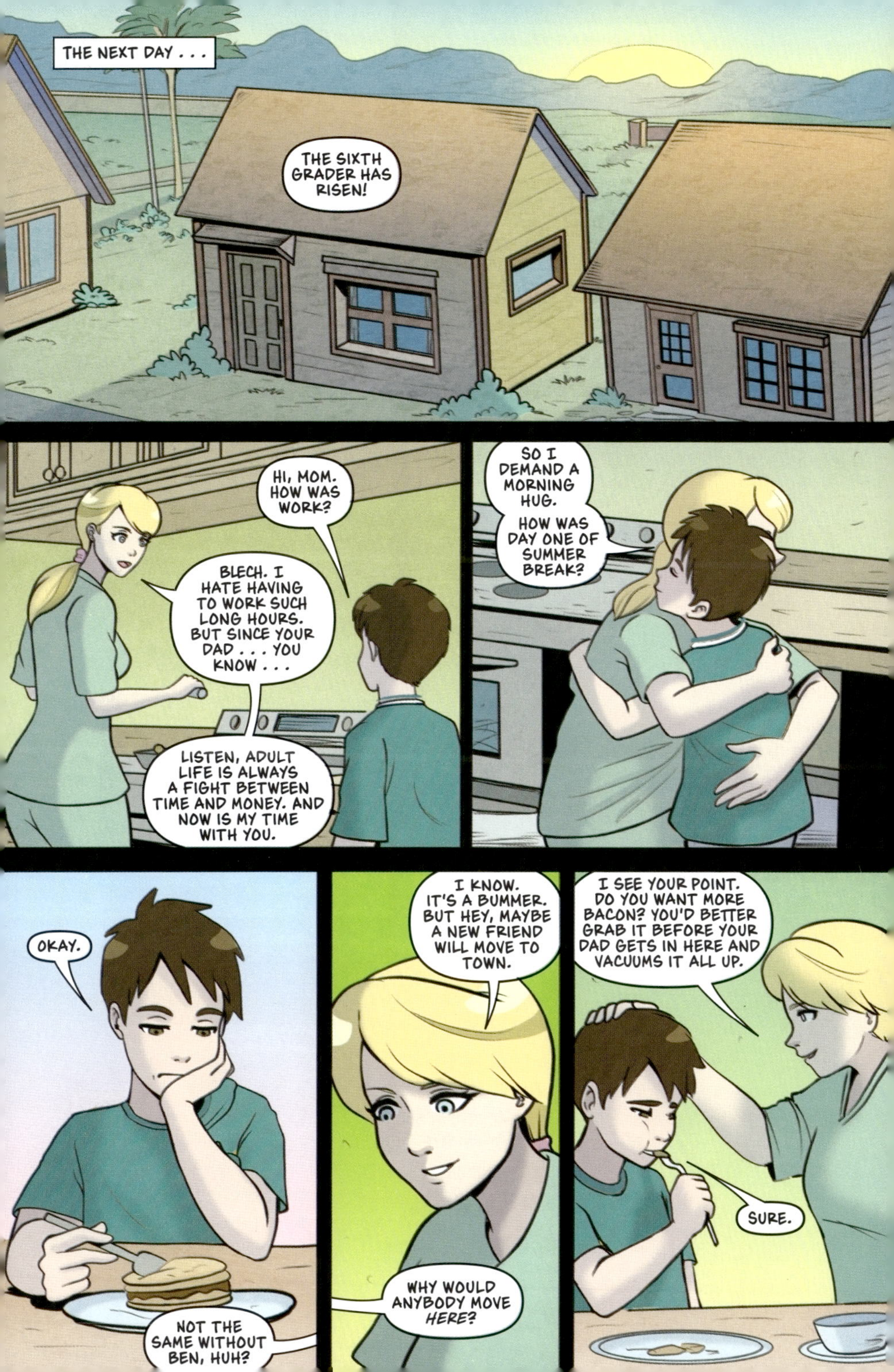
THE NEXT DAY . . .
THE SIXTH GRADER HAS RISEN!
HI, MOM. HOW WAS WORK?
BLECH. I HATE HAVING TO WORK SUCH LONG HOURS. BUT SINCE YOUR DAD . . . YOU KNOW . . .
LISTEN, ADULT LIFE IS ALWAYS A FIGHT BETWEEN TIME AND MONEY. AND NOW IS MY TIME WITH YOU.
SO I DEMAND A MORNING HUG.
HOW WAS DAY ONE OF SUMMER BREAK?
OKAY.
NOT THE SAME WITHOUT BEN, HUH?
I KNOW. IT'S A BUMMER. BUT HEY, MAYBE A NEW FRIEND WILL MOVE TO TOWN.
WHY WOULD ANYBODY MOVE HERE?
I SEE YOUR POINT. DO YOU WANT MORE BACON? YOU'D BETTER GRAB IT BEFORE YOUR DAD GETS IN HERE AND VACUUMS IT ALL UP.
SURE.

THE SUMMER GOES ON . . .

AND ON . . .
ISN'T THERE ANOTHER BOOK IN THIS SERIES?
THERE IS, BUT IT HAS A THIRTY-PERSON WAIT LIST. YOU COULD JUST BUY IT FROM THE BOOKSTORE?

END OF FREE LEVELS.
PURCHASE GEMS TO CONTINUE.
$5 10 gems
$10 25 gems
$50 Unlimited gems
AND ON . . .

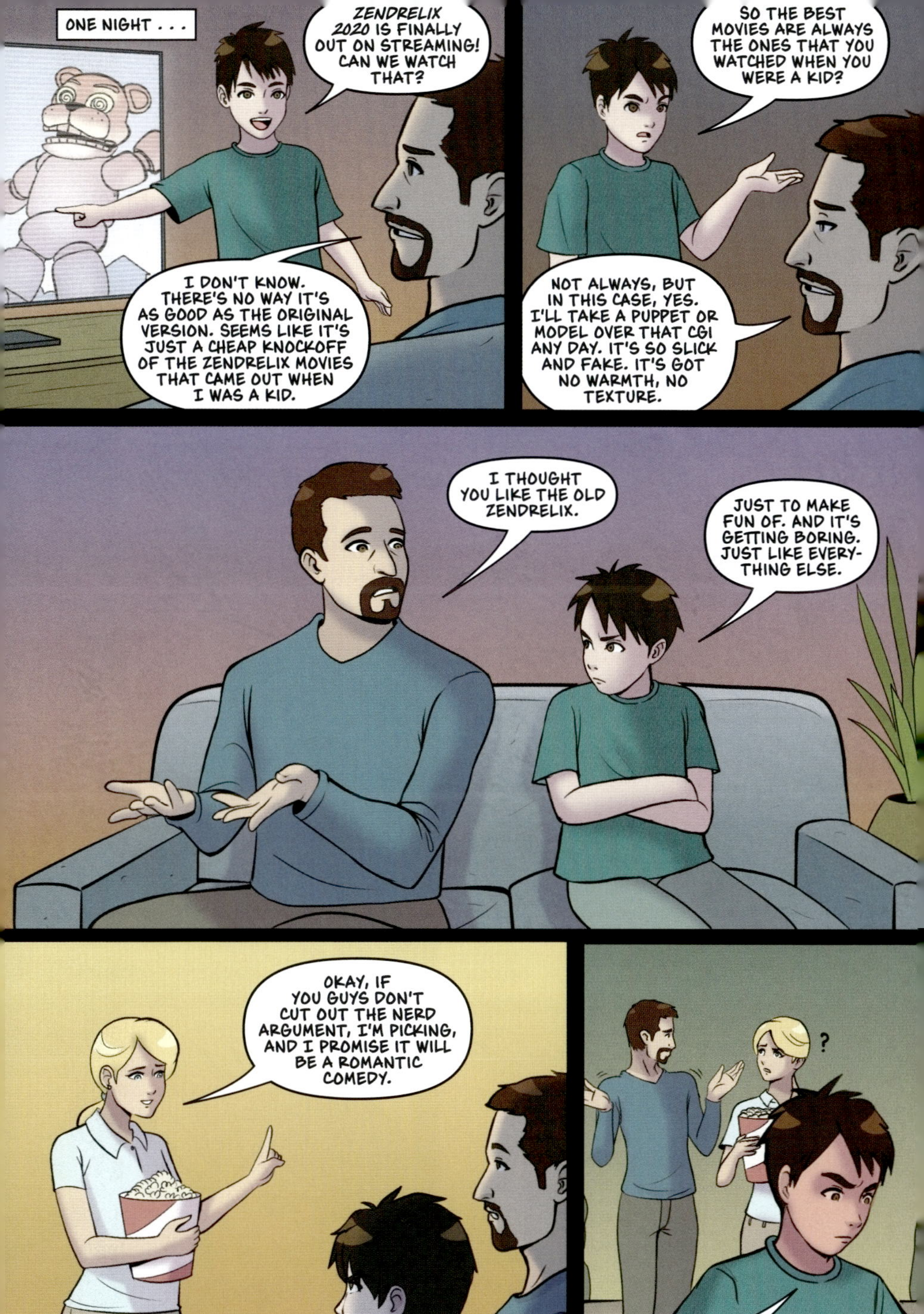

ONE NIGHT . . .
ZENDRELIX 2020 IS FINALLY OUT ON STREAMING! CAN WE WATCH THAT?
I DON'T KNOW. THERE'S NO WAY IT'S AS GOOD AS THE ORIGINAL VERSION. SEEMS LIKE IT'S JUST A CHEAP KNOCKOFF OF THE ZENDRELIX MOVIES THAT CAME OUT WHEN I WAS A KID.
SO THE BEST MOVIES ARE ALWAYS THE ONES THAT YOU WATCHED WHEN YOU WERE A KID?
NOT ALWAYS, BUT IN THIS CASE, YES. I'LL TAKE A PUPPET OR MODEL OVER THAT CGI ANY DAY. IT'S SO SLICK AND FAKE. IT'S GOT NO WARMTH, NO TEXTURE.
I THOUGHT YOU LIKE THE OLD ZENDRELIX.
JUST TO MAKE FUN OF. AND IT'S GETTING BORING. JUST LIKE EVERY-THING ELSE.
OKAY, IF YOU GUYS DON'T CUT OUT THE NERD ARGUMENT, I'M PICKING, AND I PROMISE IT WILL BE A ROMANTIC COMEDY.
?
I'M JUST GOING TO GO TO MY ROOM. WATCH WHATEVER YOU WANT.

OSWALD:
Heyback. Hows your summer?

BEN:
Awesome. At Myrtle Beach for vacation. Its so cool. Arcades and minigolf everywhere.

OSWALD:
Jealous

BEN:
Wish you were here

OSWALD:
Me too

BEN:
Hows you summer?

OSWALD:
Ok. Been going to the library a lot, lunch at Jeff's Pizza.

BEN:
That's all?

OSWALD:
Pretty much, yeah.

BEN:
I'm sorry

BEN:
That pizza place is creepy.

. . . SO THAT OLD JOHN DEERE, WELL SHE TOOK MY HEART . . .

. . . AND NOW THAT TRACTOR, SHE REFUSE TO START-
CLICK

WHAT'S WITH THE ATTITUDE, SON? I CAN TELL SOMETHING'S BEEN BOTHERING YOU, AND I KNOW IT'S NOT JUST THE COUNTRY MUSIC.

I'M TIRED OF EVERY DAY BEING EXACTLY THE SAME. BEN TEXTED ME YESTERDAY. HE'S AT MYRTLE BEACH HAVING AN AWESOME TIME.
HE WANTED TO KNOW WHAT I WAS DOING, AND I TOLD HIM I WAS GOING TO THE LIBRARY AND JEFF'S PIZZA EVERY DAY, AND YOU KNOW WHAT HE TEXTED BACK?
"I'M SORRY.
"THAT PIZZA PLACE IS CREEPY."

YEAH . . . I'M SORRY, OZ. THINGS ARE HARD RIGHT NOW WHERE MONEY'S CONCERNED.
I'M SORRY IT AFFECTS YOU. YOU'RE A KID. YOU SHOULDN'T HAVE TO WORRY ABOUT MONEY. I'M HOPING THEY'LL MOVE ME TO FULL-TIME AT THE STORE IN THE FALL.
THAT'LL HELP A LOT, AND IF I GET PROMOTED TO DELI MANAGER, IT'LL BE ANOTHER DOLLAR FIFTY AN HOUR.

BEN'S DAD GOT A JOB THAT PAYS EVEN BETTER THAN HIS OLD JOB AT THE MILL.

BEN'S DAD HAD TO MOVE FIVE HUNDRED MILES AWAY TO GET THAT JOB.
YOUR MOM AND I TALKED A LOT ABOUT IT, BUT WE DECIDED NOT TO MOVE, ESPECIALLY WITH YOUR GRANDMA LIVING HERE AND NEEDING HELP SOMETIMES.
THIS IS OUR HOME, KIDDO, AND THINGS AREN'T PERFECT, BUT WE JUST HAVE TO MAKE THE BEST OF THEM.
AND SO EVERY DAY YOU TOSS ME OUT ON THE STREET LIKE I'M GARBAGE. IF THIS IS THE BEST OF THINGS, I'D HATE TO SEE THE WORST!
SLAM

2:32
ALMOST TIME FOR PICKUP.
DO NOT USE
UNLESS . . .
NO, TODAY'S GOING TO BE DIFFERENT.
TODAY YOU HAVE TO COME IN AND FIND ME.
DO NOT USE

YOU'RE NOT DROPPING ME OFF AND PICKING ME UP LIKE SOMEBODY'S DRY CLEANING TODAY.
DO NOT USE
AND I'M NOT GOING TO MAKE IT EASY FOR YOU . . .
EVEN IF IT MEANS I GET PINK EYE IN HERE.

ACHOO!
I DON'T KNOW IF DAD'S LOOKING FOR ME YET, BUT THAT PROBABLY JUST GAVE ME AWAY.
BESIDES, I NEED AIR . . .
BEEP BOOP
DING DING DING
HA HA HA HA!
YAY!
WHAT . . .

SPACE
WIN
!!!
TOTO, I DON'T THINK WE'RE IN KANSAS ANYMORE.

FREDDY FAZBEAR'S PIZZA
WHERE AM I?
FREDDY FAZBEAR'S PIZZA
IT CAN'T BE . . .
THIS IS WHAT JEFF'S PIZZA USED TO BE!
AND THOSE . . .
LET'S EAT!!!
. . . LOOK JUST LIKE THE THINGS I'VE BEEN DRAWING LATELY.
BUT CREEPIER.
AH!
SORRY, DUDE. YOU OKAY?

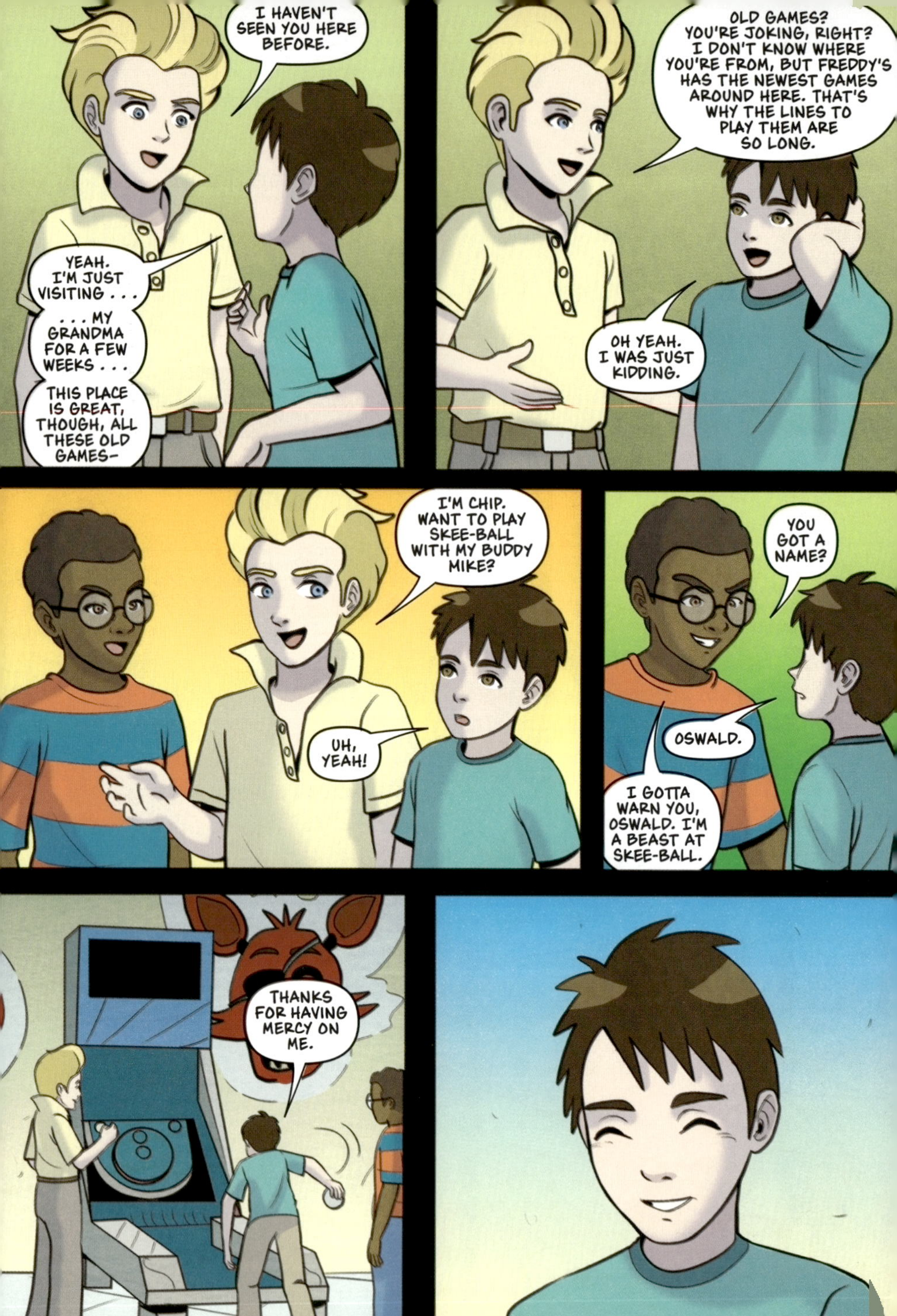
I HAVEN'T SEEN YOU HERE BEFORE.
YEAH. I'M JUST VISITING . . .
. . . MY GRANDMA FOR A FEW WEEKS . . .
THIS PLACE IS GREAT, THOUGH, ALL THESE OLD GAMES-
OLD GAMES? YOU'RE JOKING, RIGHT? I DON'T KNOW WHERE YOU'RE FROM, BUT FREDDY'S HAS THE NEWEST GAMES AROUND HERE. THAT'S WHY THE LINES TO PLAY THEM ARE SO LONG.
OH YEAH. I WAS JUST KIDDING.
I'M CHIP. WANT TO PLAY SKEE-BALL WITH MY BUDDY MIKE?
UH, YEAH!
YOU GOT A NAME?
OSWALD.
I GOTTA WARN YOU, OSWALD. I'M A BEAST AT SKEE-BALL.
THANKS FOR HAVING MERCY ON ME.

A LITTLE LATER . . .

HEY, GUYS . . .

I'D . . . BETTER RUN. MY GRANDMA'S SUPPOSED TO PICK ME UP IN A FEW MINUTES.
OKAY, DUDE, MAYBE WE'LL CATCH YOU LATER.

NOW . . . HOW DO I GET BACK? PROBABLY NOT JUST THE FRONT DOOR.
NOT LIKE DAD'S IN THE CAR WAITING OUTSIDE HERE IN THE '80S.

I'LL TRY THE WAY I CAME IN, I GUESS . . .

I DON'T HEAR ANYTHING ANYMORE . . .
JEFF'S
IT WORKED!
NOW TO FIND OUT HOW MUCH TROUBLE I'M IN-
NO TIME'S PASSED HERE AT ALL . . .
SEE YA, KID!

YOU'RE IN A GOOD MOOD TODAY. QUITE A CONTRAST FROM YESTERDAY'S MR. GRUMPY PANTS.

IT'S JUST BECAUSE I DISCOVERED A BALL PIT AT JEFF'S PIZZA THAT LETS ME TRAVEL IN TIME . . .
WHAT WAS THAT?
OH, I SAID THE LIBRARY IS SUPPOSED TO GET MY BOOK IN TODAY.

READY TO GO, OZ?
READY!

BYE, DAD!
GLAD YOU'RE FEELING BETTER, SON.
UH-HUH!

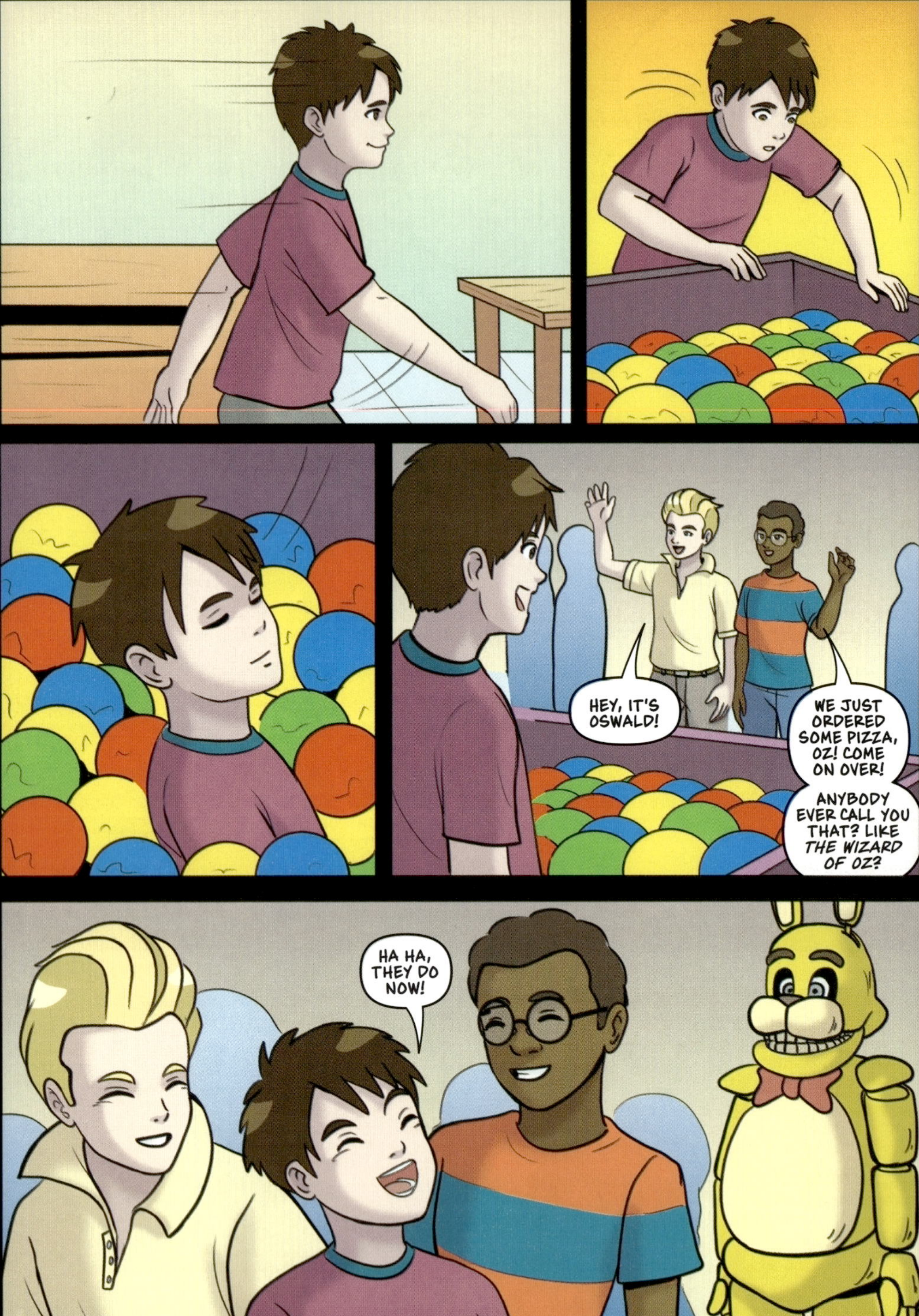
HEY, IT'S OSWALD!
WE JUST ORDERED SOME PIZZA, OZ! COME ON OVER!
ANYBODY EVER CALL YOU THAT? LIKE *THE WIZARD OF OZ*?
HA HA, THEY DO NOW!

LET'S EAT!!!
YOU KNOW, WHEN I WAS LITTLE, I LOVED FREDDY FAZBEAR'S BAND. I EVEN HAD A STUFFED FREDDY I USED TO SLEEP WITH.
NOW I LOOK UP AT THAT STAGE, AND THOSE THINGS GIVE ME THE CREEPS.
IT'S WEIRD, HUH? HOW STUFF YOU LIKED AS A LITTLE KID GETS CREEPY WHEN YOU'RE OLDER?
LIKE CLOWNS.
YEAH, OR DOLLS. SOMETIMES I THINK THE DOLLS ALL LINED UP IN MY SISTER'S ROOM ARE STARING AT ME.
OR RABBITS . . .

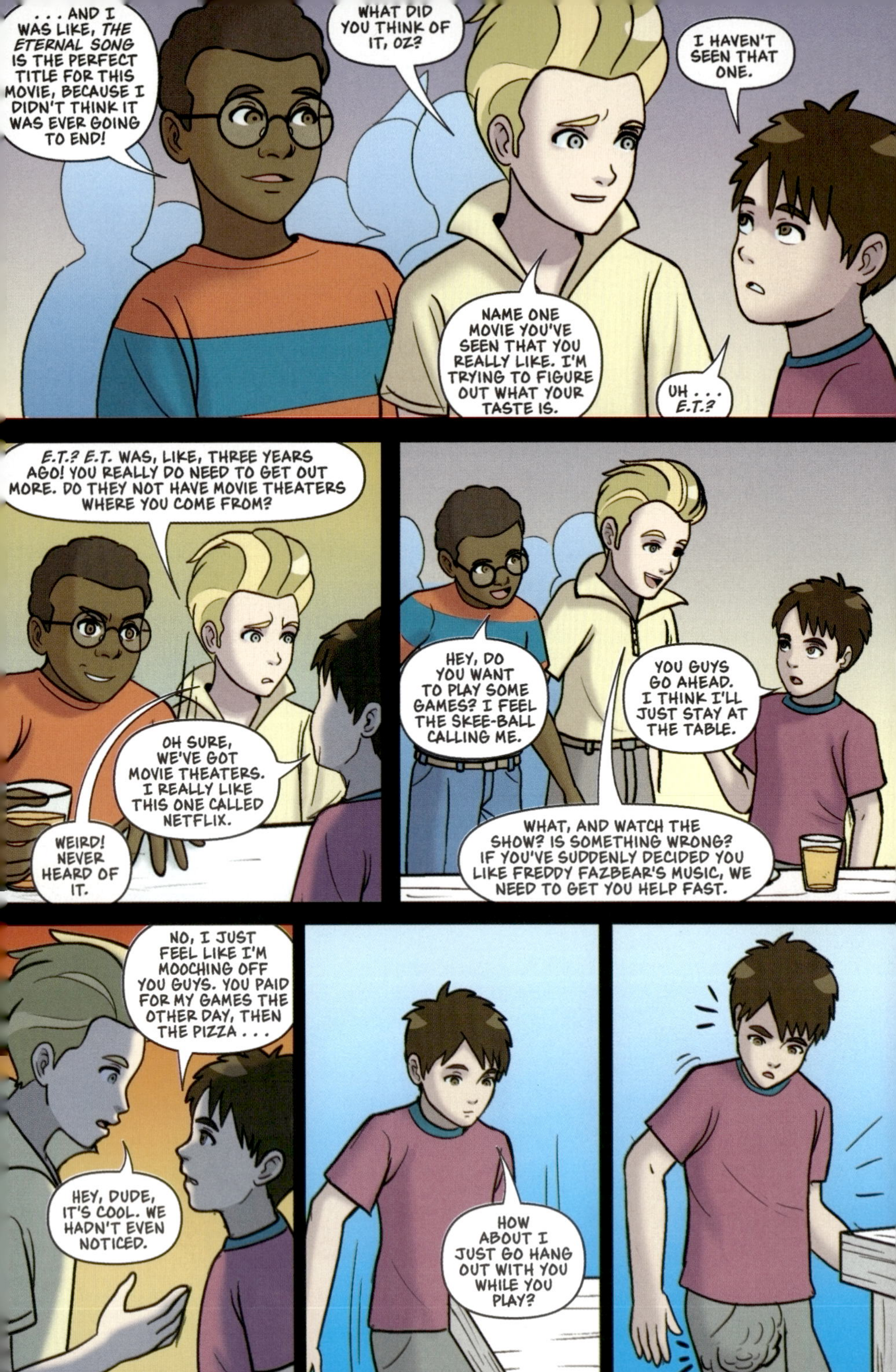
. . . AND I WAS LIKE, *THE ETERNAL SONG* IS THE PERFECT TITLE FOR THIS MOVIE, BECAUSE I DIDN'T THINK IT WAS EVER GOING TO END!
WHAT DID YOU THINK OF IT, OZ?
I HAVEN'T SEEN THAT ONE.
NAME ONE MOVIE YOU'VE SEEN THAT YOU REALLY LIKE. I'M TRYING TO FIGURE OUT WHAT YOUR TASTE IS.
UH . . . *E.T.?*
E.T.? E.T. WAS, LIKE, THREE YEARS AGO! YOU REALLY DO NEED TO GET OUT MORE. DO THEY NOT HAVE MOVIE THEATERS WHERE YOU COME FROM?
OH SURE, WE'VE GOT MOVIE THEATERS. I REALLY LIKE THIS ONE CALLED NETFLIX.
WEIRD! NEVER HEARD OF IT.
HEY, DO YOU WANT TO PLAY SOME GAMES? I FEEL THE SKEE-BALL CALLING ME.
YOU GUYS GO AHEAD. I THINK I'LL JUST STAY AT THE TABLE.
WHAT, AND WATCH THE SHOW? IS SOMETHING WRONG? IF YOU'VE SUDDENLY DECIDED YOU LIKE FREDDY FAZBEAR'S MUSIC, WE NEED TO GET YOU HELP FAST.
NO, I JUST FEEL LIKE I'M MOOCHING OFF YOU GUYS. YOU PAID FOR MY GAMES THE OTHER DAY, THEN THE PIZZA . . .
HEY, DUDE, IT'S COOL. WE HADN'T EVEN NOTICED.
HOW ABOUT I JUST GO HANG OUT WITH YOU WHILE YOU PLAY?

OR WE COULD PLAY USING THESE?
I GUESS . . .
. . . I FORGOT I WAS WEARING THESE PANTS THAT HAD ALL THE TOKENS IN THEM?
HA HA HA, YEAH, THAT'LL WORK, OZ! LET'S GO!
YOU'RE CRAZY, DUDE.
HEH, YEP! THAT'S ME, I GUESS!

THE NEXT DAY . . .
DAD, HOW OLD WERE YOU IN 1985?
I WAS JUST A COUPLE YEARS OLDER THAN YOU.
AND OTHER THAN BASEBALL, ALL I COULD THINK ABOUT WAS HOW MANY QUARTERS I HAD TO SPEND AT THE ARCADE. WHY DO YOU ASK?
I'VE JUST BEEN DOING SOME RESEARCH. JEFF'S PIZZA, BACK BEFORE IT WAS JEFF'S PIZZA . . .
. . . IT WAS SOME KIND OF ARCADE, WASN'T IT?
YEAH, IT WAS.
. . .
BUT IT CLOSED.
LIKE EVERYTHING ELSE IN THIS TOWN.
PRETTY MUCH, YEAH.

HAVE A GOOD DAY, SON. SEE YOU IN THE AFTERNOON.
WHAT WAS THAT ABOUT?
JEFF'S IN THE BACK . . .

AAAAAAAAAAAAH!!
HUH?
AAAAAAAAAA!!
SUSIE?! SUSIE, WHERE ARE YOU?!
SOMEBODY HELP!
SOMETHING'S NOT RIGHT.
CHIP? MIKE?
WELL, I CAN'T BE IN DANGER HERE, BECAUSE THIS IS THE PAST.
AND IF I HAVEN'T EVEN BEEN BORN YET . . .
PRIVATE
. . . NOTHING BAD CAN HAPPEN TO ME–
WHAT?
FOLLOW YOU?
THIS IS THE WORST VERSION OF *ALICE IN WONDERLAND* I'VE EVER SEEN . . .

YOU CAN'T HURT ME . . .
PARTY ROOM
PARTY ROOM
I HAVEN'T BEEN BORN . . .
YOU CAN'T . . .
. . . HURT . . .

AAAAAAAAAAH!!!
PARTY ROOM

. . . HE DIDN'T COME IN FOR HIS USUAL SLICE AND A SODA TODAY . . .
OKAY, WELL, IF HE COMES IN, HAVE HIM CALL ME, PLEASE . . .
DAD?
WHAT WERE YOU THINKING, HIDING IN THAT NASTY OLD THING?
DIDN'T YOU HEAR ME CALLING YOU?
I. . .
TIME . . . MOVED THIS . . . TIME?
WHAT ARE YOU TALKING ABOUT?

LOOK HOW DIRTY THIS IS. YOUR MOTHER-

DAD!!
MMMPH!
!
JEFF?!

WHAT ARE YOU–
HELP! JEFF, HELP!
SEE YOU LATER, GUYS.
JEFF?

WHAT . . .
WHAT DID YOU DO TO MY DAD?
. . .
WHERE ARE YOU TAKING ME?
HOME?!
HOW DO YOU KNOW WHERE I LIVE?!

YOU CAN'T DO THIS. THIS-
THIS IS KIDNAPPING OR SOMETHING!
HSSSSSSS!!!
MY MOM WILL BE HOME SOON, AND SHE'LL CALL THE POLICE.

I'M GOING TO MY ROOM NOW, OKAY?
I'M NOT TRYING TO ESCAPE. I'M JUST GOING TO MY ROOM.
tap tap
Mom, emergency! Somethings wrong with dad.
Come home now!

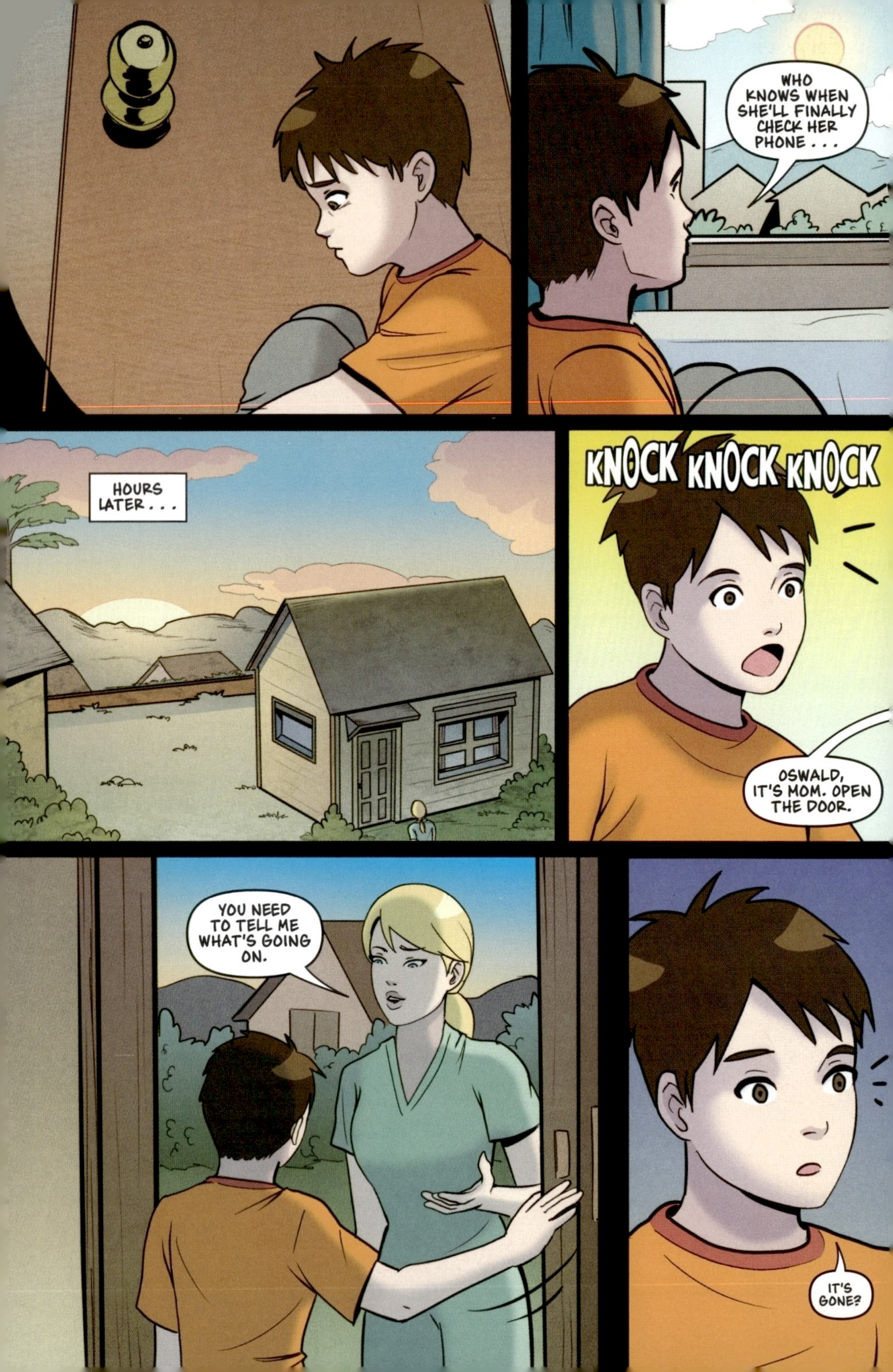

WHO KNOWS WHEN SHE'LL FINALLY CHECK HER PHONE . . .

HOURS LATER . . .

KNOCK KNOCK KNOCK

OSWALD, IT'S MOM. OPEN THE DOOR.

YOU NEED TO TELL ME WHAT'S GOING ON.

IT'S GONE?

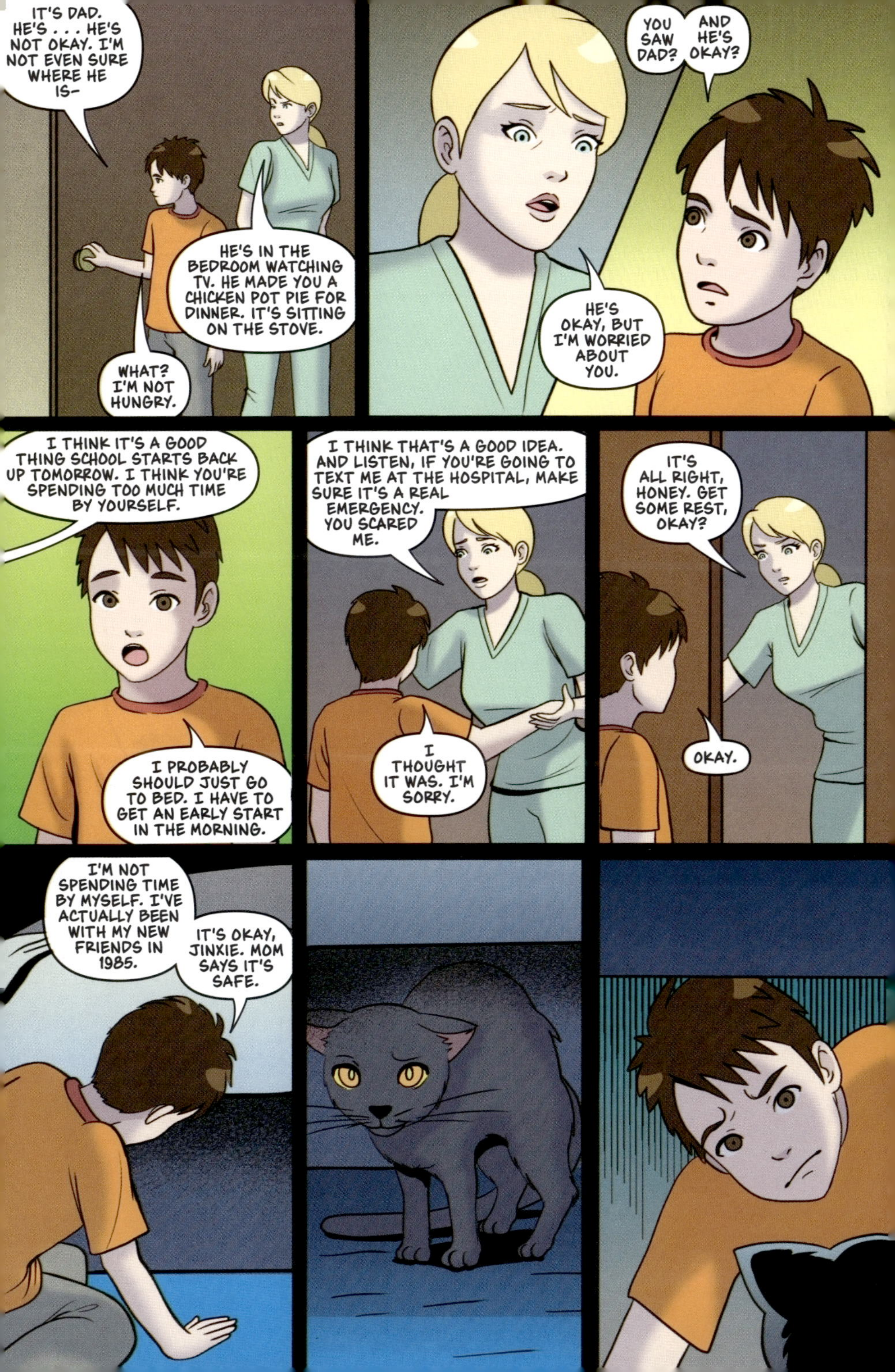

IT'S DAD. HE'S . . . HE'S NOT OKAY. I'M NOT EVEN SURE WHERE HE IS–

HE'S IN THE BEDROOM WATCHING TV. HE MADE YOU A CHICKEN POT PIE FOR DINNER. IT'S SITTING ON THE STOVE.

WHAT? I'M NOT HUNGRY.

YOU SAW DAD?

AND HE'S OKAY?

HE'S OKAY, BUT I'M WORRIED ABOUT YOU.

I THINK IT'S A GOOD THING SCHOOL STARTS BACK UP TOMORROW. I THINK YOU'RE SPENDING TOO MUCH TIME BY YOURSELF.

I PROBABLY SHOULD JUST GO TO BED. I HAVE TO GET AN EARLY START IN THE MORNING.

I THINK THAT'S A GOOD IDEA. AND LISTEN, IF YOU'RE GOING TO TEXT ME AT THE HOSPITAL, MAKE SURE IT'S A REAL EMERGENCY. YOU SCARED ME.

I THOUGHT IT WAS. I'M SORRY.

IT'S ALL RIGHT, HONEY. GET SOME REST, OKAY?

OKAY.

THE NEXT MORNING . . .
OH . . . THAT SMELLS GOOD.
WAS IT A . . .
. . . DREAM?
MAYBE JUST FORGET IT ALL. NEW SCHOOL YEAR. NEW BEGINNING.
FEELING BETTER?
YEAH, I'M PRETTY . . .
. . . HUNGRY.

UH . . . MOM?
WHAT IS IT, HON?
WHERE'S DAD?
OSWALD, YOUR DAD IS SITTING RIGHT THERE! IF THIS IS SOME KIND OF ELABORATE PRANK, YOU CAN CUT IT OUT RIGHT NOW, BECAUSE IT HAS OFFICIALLY STOPPED BEING FUNNY.
OKAY, I UNDERSTAND. I'LL CUT IT OUT. I APOLOGIZE.
DON'T DALLY TOO LONG. YOUR DAD'S TAKING YOU TO SCHOOL BEFORE WORK, AND NEITHER OF YOU WANT TO BE LATE.

I DON'T UNDERSTAND. ARE YOU REAL? IS THIS REAL? AM I GOING CRAZY?
DON'T BOTHER PICKING ME UP THIS AFTERNOON. I'LL JUST CATCH THE BUS.

LATER THAT DAY . . .
DO YOU MIND IF I SHARE YOUR BENCH?
SURE, HELP YOURSELF.
WHAT ARE YOU READING?
GREEK MYTHOLOGY. I'VE PROBABLY READ THIS BOOK A DOZEN TIMES. IT'S LIKE A COMFORT BOOK FOR ME. I READ IT WHEN I NEED TO BE BRAVE.
WHY'S THAT?
WELL, THE GREEK HEROES ARE SUPER BRAVE. THEY'RE ALWAYS DOING BATTLE WITH SOME KIND OF BIG MONSTER, LIKE THE MINOTAUR OR HYDRA.
IT KIND OF PUTS THINGS IN PERSPECTIVE, YOU KNOW?
NO MATTER HOW BAD MY PROBLEMS ARE, AT LEAST I DON'T HAVE TO BATTLE WITH A MONSTER.
LIKE A GIANT YELLOW RABBIT . . .

WHAT?
NOTHING. SO YOU READ THAT BOOK WHEN YOU NEED TO BE BRAVE . . .
FIRST DAY AT A NEW SCHOOL, THIRD DAY IN A NEW TOWN. I DON'T KNOW ANYBODY YET.
YES, YOU DO.
I'M OSWALD.
I'M GABRIELLE.
THANKS, GABRIELLE. THIS IS EXACTLY THE CONVERSATION I NEEDED TO HAVE TODAY.

THAT NIGHT . . .
AREN'T YOU GOING TO EAT ANYTHING . . . DAD?
OKAY, WELL. I'M GOING TO GET A GLASS OF MILK AND DO MY HOMEWORK NOW.
HERE YOU GO, JINXIE. IT'S OKAY. . .
OR IT WILL BE, SOON.
I HOPE.

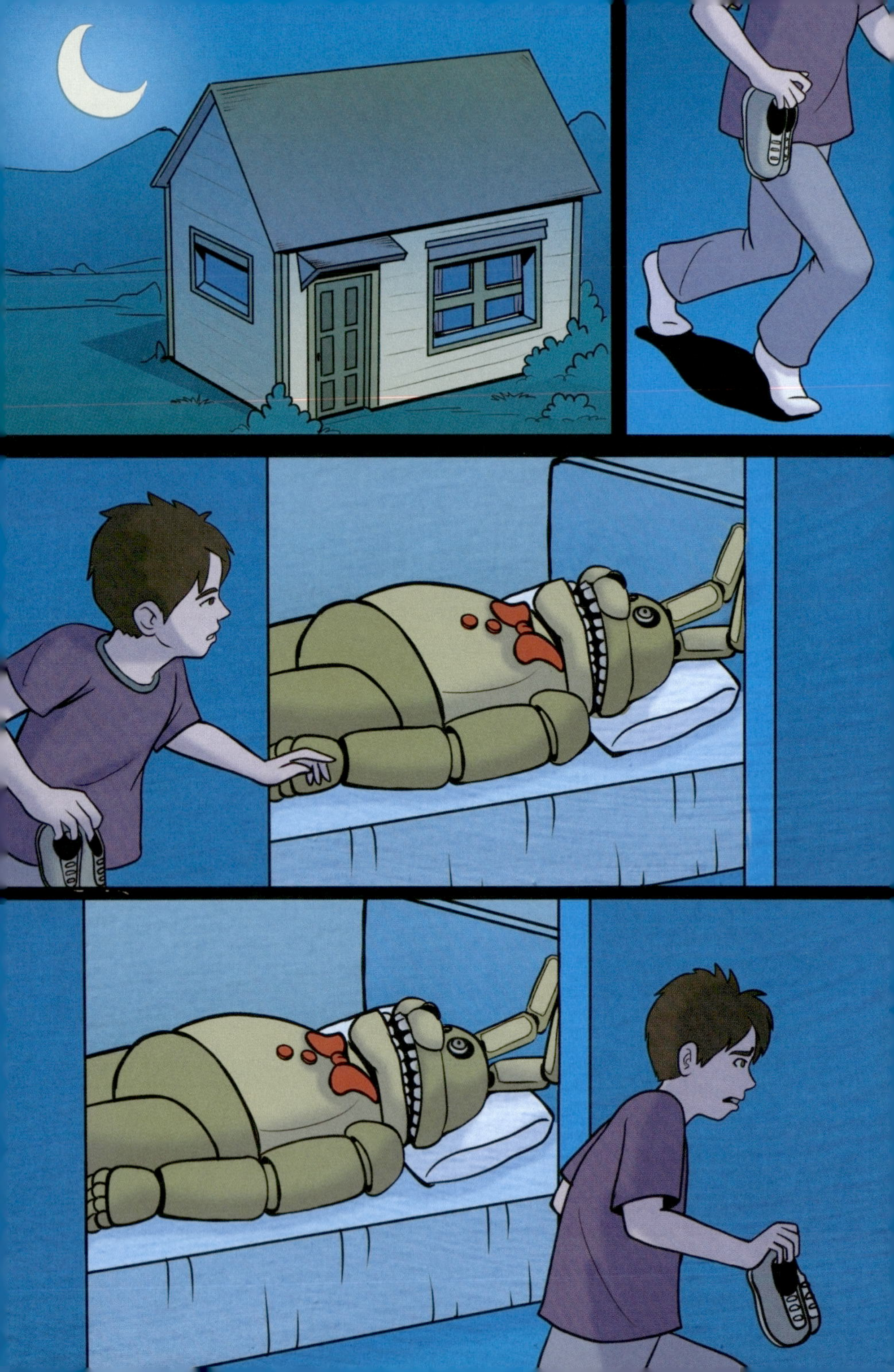

JEFF'S PIZZA

H-HI, JEFF . . .
OH, HEY.
YOU KNOW, WE JUST SERVE WHOLE PIZZAS AT NIGHT. NO SLICES.
YEAH, I JUST STOPPED BY TO GET A SODA TO GO.
OKAY . . .
LET ME GET A PIE OUT OF THE OVEN, THEN I'LL GET IT FOR YOU. ORANGE, RIGHT?
RIGHT. THANKS.
COME ON . . .

DAD! YOU'RE STILL HERE! OH, PLEASE BE ALIVE.
YOU HAVE TO BE . . .

HE'S BREATHING . . .
THANK GOODNESS.
AND WE'RE NOT IN THE '80S . . .
BUT HOW DO I GET YOU OUT OF HERE?
I CAN'T CALL MOM. SHE'LL JUST THINK I'M CRAZY OR LYING AGAIN-
AH!
NO!

WHACK
THUNK

ARRGHH!

AAAH!
WHAT KIND OF RABBIT HAS FANGS, YOU FREAK?!
NO!
LEAVE . . .
. . . MY DAD . . .

ALONE!

GREEK HEROES . . .
BE BRAVE . . .

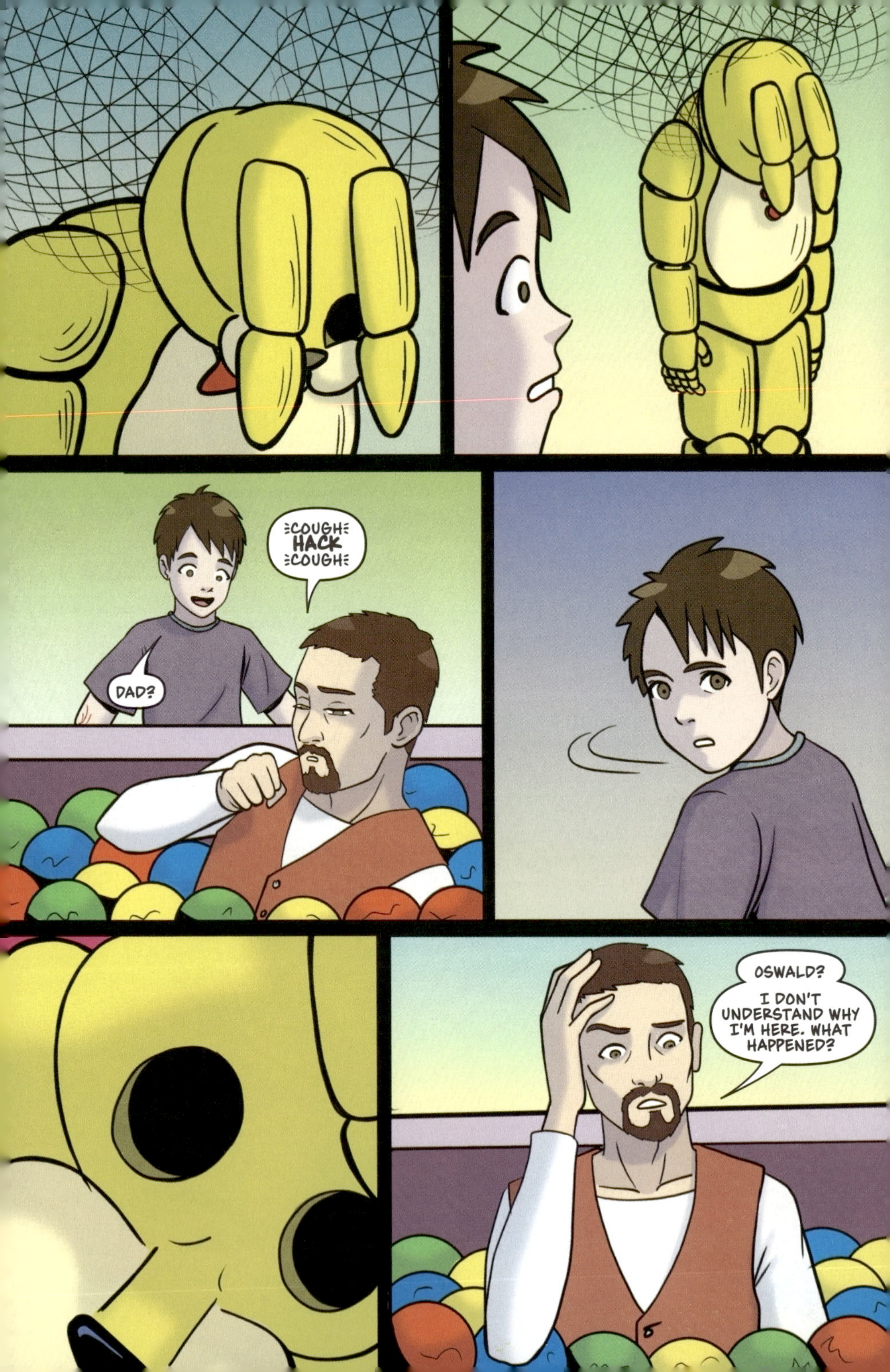
DAD?
COUGH
HACK
COUGH
OSWALD?
I DON'T UNDERSTAND WHY I'M HERE. WHAT HAPPENED?

UH . . .

I HID IN THE BALL PIT TO PLAY A PRANK ON YOU . . .
WHICH I SHOULDN'T HAVE DONE!
YOU CAME TO LOOK FOR ME, AND I GUESS YOU MUST'VE HIT YOUR HEAD AND LOST CONSCIOUSNESS.

I'M SORRY, DAD. I DIDN'T MEAN FOR THINGS TO GET SO OUT OF HAND.
I ACCEPT YOUR APOLOGY, SON . . .

BUT YOU'RE RIGHT. YOU SHOULDN'T HAVE DONE IT. AND JEFF REALLY SHOULD GET RID OF THIS BALL PIT BEFORE HE HAS A LAWSUIT ON HIS HANDS.
I AGREE.

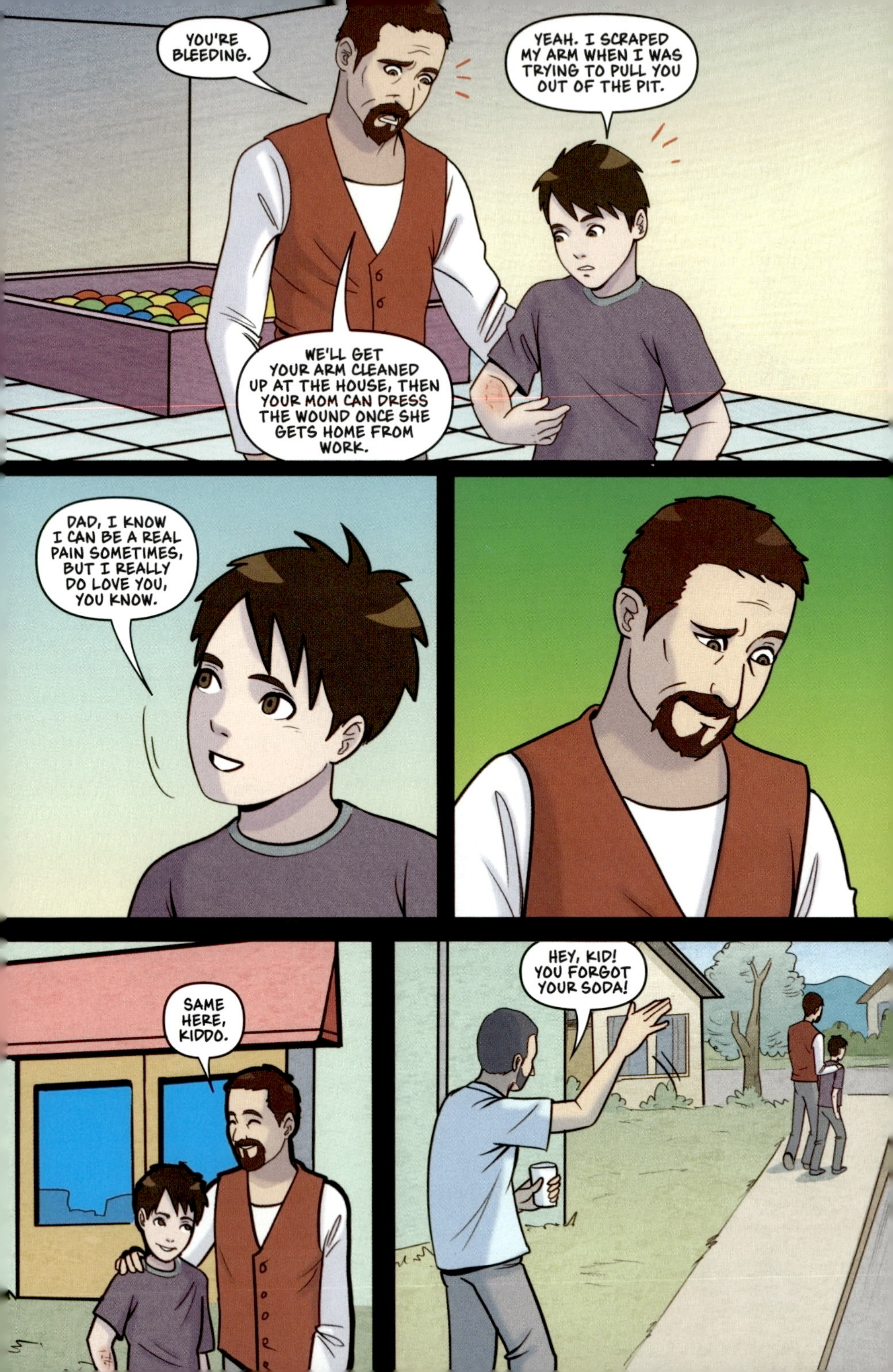
YOU'RE BLEEDING.
YEAH. I SCRAPED MY ARM WHEN I WAS TRYING TO PULL YOU OUT OF THE PIT.
WE'LL GET YOUR ARM CLEANED UP AT THE HOUSE, THEN YOUR MOM CAN DRESS THE WOUND ONCE SHE GETS HOME FROM WORK.
DAD, I KNOW I CAN BE A REAL PAIN SOMETIMES, BUT I REALLY DO LOVE YOU, YOU KNOW.
SAME HERE, KIDDO.
HEY, KID! YOU FORGOT YOUR SODA!

TO BE BEAUTIFUL

CHANGE OUT THE BODY PARTS INTO COUNTLESS HILARIOUS COMBINATIONS! DIFFERENT EYES!
DIFFERENT MOUTHS!
BIG NOSES!
WACKY EARS!
IT'S MRS. MIX-AND-MATCH!
IT'S MRS. MIX-AND-MATCH.
AT LEAST THE DOLL HAS A HUSBAND.

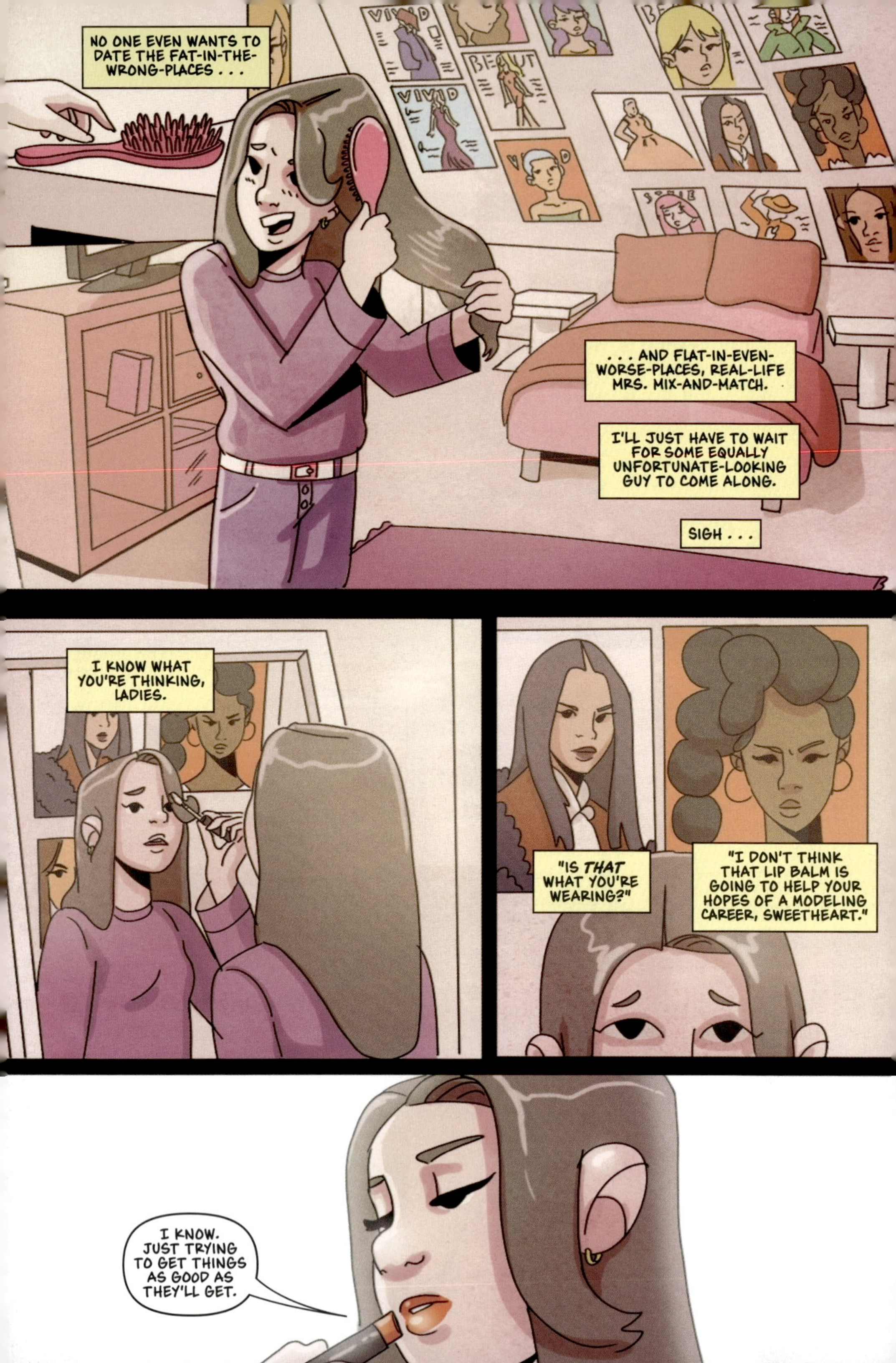
NO ONE EVEN WANTS TO DATE THE FAT-IN-THE-WRONG-PLACES . . .
. . . AND FLAT-IN-EVEN-WORSE-PLACES, REAL-LIFE MRS. MIX-AND-MATCH.
I'LL JUST HAVE TO WAIT FOR SOME EQUALLY UNFORTUNATE-LOOKING GUY TO COME ALONG.
SIGH . . .
I KNOW WHAT YOU'RE THINKING, LADIES.
"IS THAT WHAT YOU'RE WEARING?"
"I DON'T THINK THAT LIP BALM IS GOING TO HELP YOUR HOPES OF A MODELING CAREER, SWEETHEART."
I KNOW. JUST TRYING TO GET THINGS AS GOOD AS THEY'LL GET.

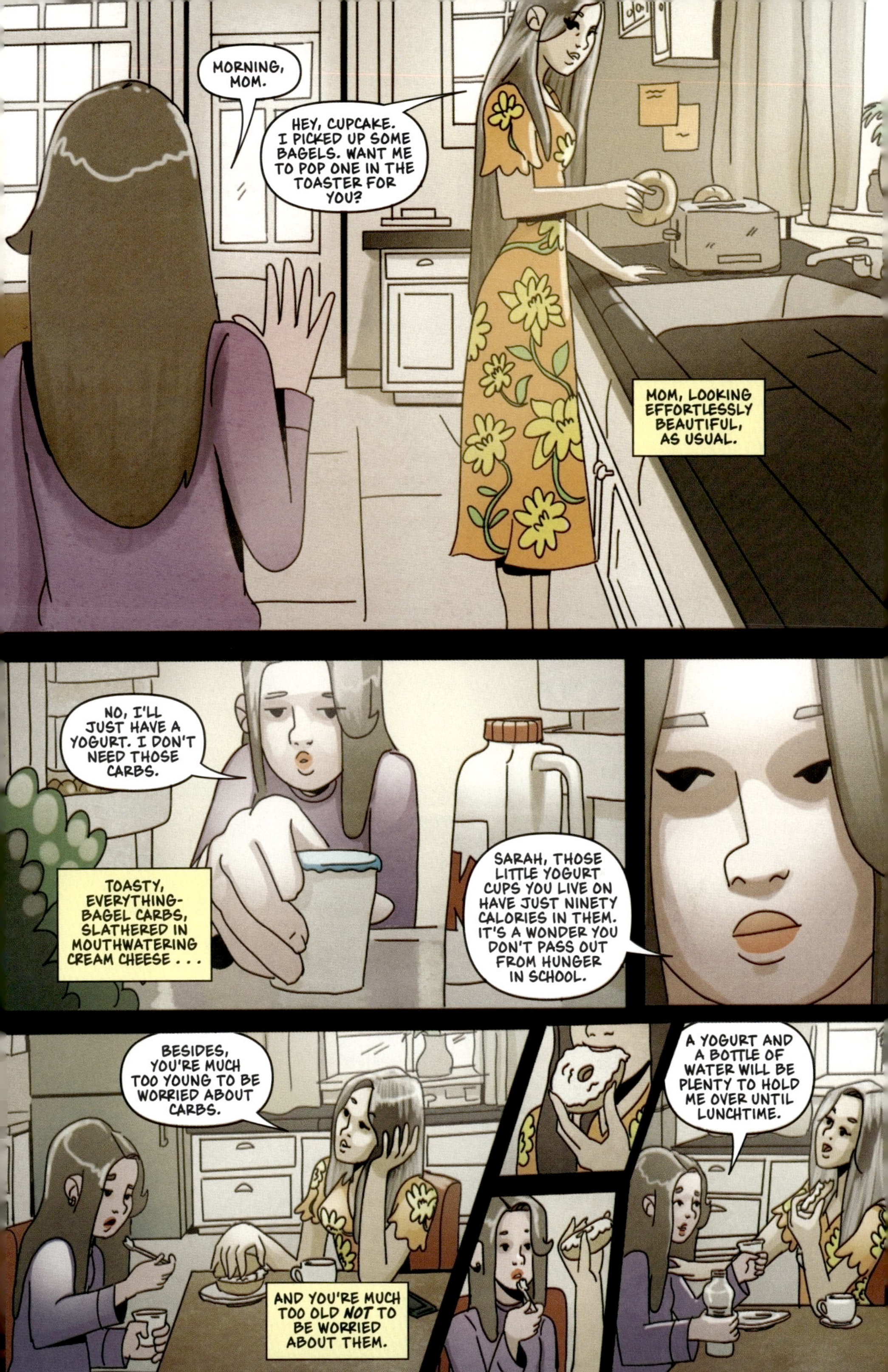
MORNING, MOM.
HEY, CUPCAKE. I PICKED UP SOME BAGELS. WANT ME TO POP ONE IN THE TOASTER FOR YOU?
MOM, LOOKING EFFORTLESSLY BEAUTIFUL, AS USUAL.
NO, I'LL JUST HAVE A YOGURT. I DON'T NEED THOSE CARBS.
TOASTY, EVERYTHING-BAGEL CARBS, SLATHERED IN MOUTHWATERING CREAM CHEESE . . .
SARAH, THOSE LITTLE YOGURT CUPS YOU LIVE ON HAVE JUST NINETY CALORIES IN THEM. IT'S A WONDER YOU DON'T PASS OUT FROM HUNGER IN SCHOOL.
BESIDES, YOU'RE MUCH TOO YOUNG TO BE WORRIED ABOUT CARBS.
AND YOU'RE MUCH TOO OLD *NOT* TO BE WORRIED ABOUT THEM.
A YOGURT AND A BOTTLE OF WATER WILL BE PLENTY TO HOLD ME OVER UNTIL LUNCHTIME.

STOP
MAYBE ON MY NEXT BIRTHDAY, MOM WILL LET ME WEAR MORE MAKEUP THAN JUST BB CREAM, MASCARA, AND TINTED LIP BALM.
AND HERE'S HOW I GET THAT FRESH-FACED LOOK . . .
I COULD DO ACTUAL CONTOURING, MAKE MY CHEEKBONES LOOK MORE PRONOUNCED, GET MY NOSE TO SEEM LESS BULBOUS.
HAVING MY EYEBROWS DONE PROFESSIONALLY WOULD ALSO REALLY HELP.
MY MEASLY TWEEZERS ARE LOSING THE BATTLE WITH THE UNIBROW–
...

THE BEAUTIFULS . . .
ROYALTY. STARS. EVERY GIRL IN SCHOOL WANTS TO BE THEM. EVERY BOY WANTS-

WHAT ARE THEY, PENGUINS?
HUH?

THEY LOOK LIKE PENGUINS! LET'S HOPE THERE AREN'T ANY HUNGRY SEALS AROUND.
ARF ARF ARF!

YOU'RE CRAZY, ABBY.
I THINK THEY LOOK PERFECT.
YOU ALWAYS DO. AND I HAVE A THEORY ABOUT WHY.
ABBY WANTS TO BE A SCIENTIST SOMEDAY. SHE ALWAYS HAS A THEORY.
YOU KNOW HOW WE USED TO PLAY BARBIES WHEN WE WERE LITTLE?
YEAH.
SHE HASN'T CHANGED MUCH SINCE THOSE DAYS. SHE STILL WEARS HER HAIR IN THE SAME BRAIDS, STILL WEARS GOLD WIRE-FRAMED GLASSES.
MY THEORY IS THAT YOU USED TO LOVE TO PLAY WITH BARBIES, BUT NOW THAT YOU'RE TOO OLD FOR THEM, YOU NEED A BARBIE SUBSTITUTE.
BUT THE OPPORTUNITY IS THERE. HER COMPLEXION IS FLAWLESS, AND HER EYES ARE A STARTLING HAZEL BEHIND THOSE GLASSES. SHE HAS A DANCER'S BODY UNDER HER BAGGY CLOTHES.
THOSE EMPTY-HEADED FASHIONISTAS ARE YOUR BARBIE SUBSTITUTE. THAT'S WHY YOU WANT TO PLAY WITH THEM.

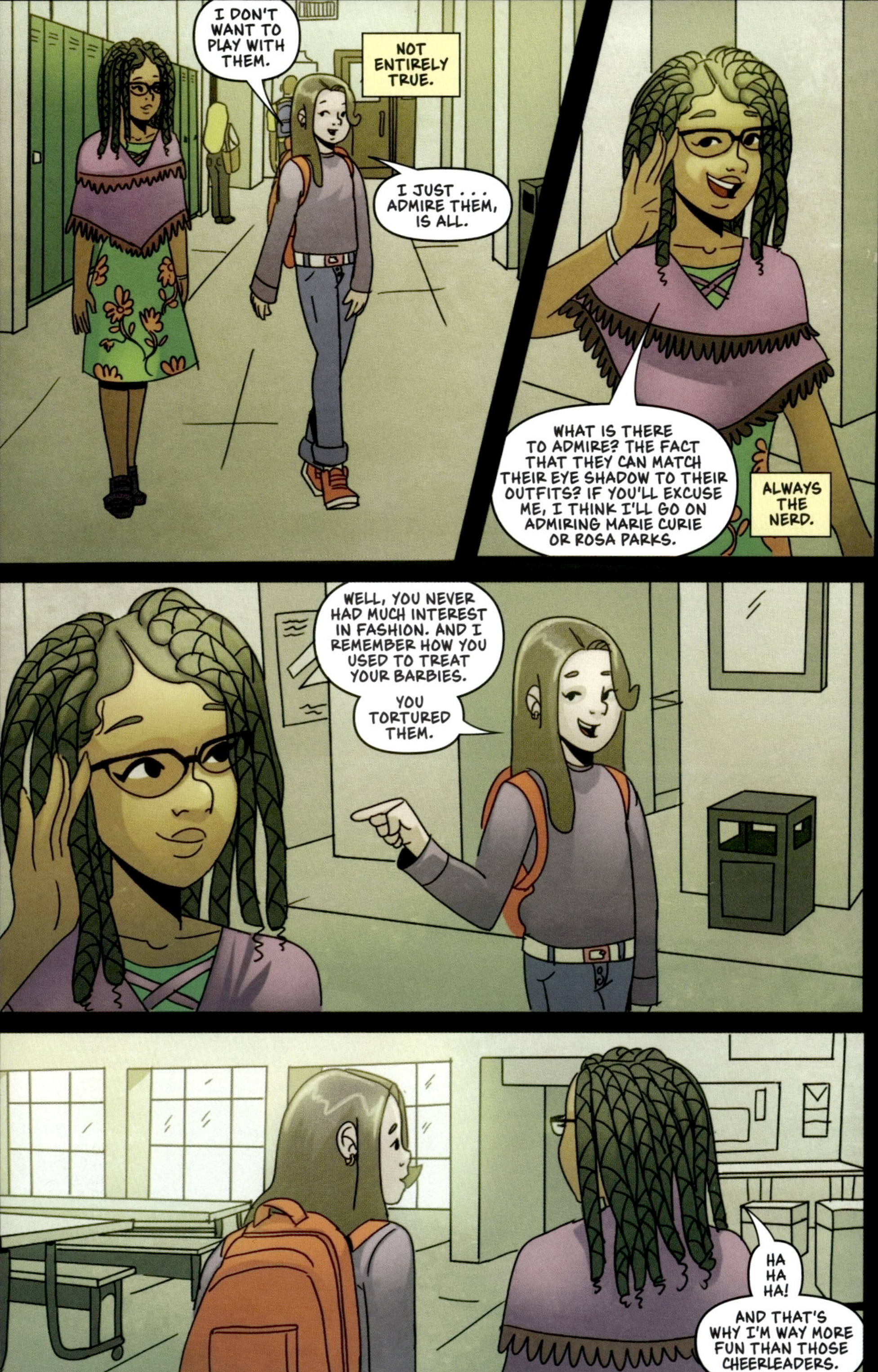
I DON'T WANT TO PLAY WITH THEM.
NOT ENTIRELY TRUE.
I JUST . . . ADMIRE THEM, IS ALL.
WHAT IS THERE TO ADMIRE? THE FACT THAT THEY CAN MATCH THEIR EYE SHADOW TO THEIR OUTFITS? IF YOU'LL EXCUSE ME, I THINK I'LL GO ON ADMIRING MARIE CURIE OR ROSA PARKS.
ALWAYS THE NERD.
WELL, YOU NEVER HAD MUCH INTEREST IN FASHION. AND I REMEMBER HOW YOU USED TO TREAT YOUR BARBIES.
YOU TORTURED THEM.
HA HA HA!
AND THAT'S WHY I'M WAY MORE FUN THAN THOSE CHEERLEADERS.

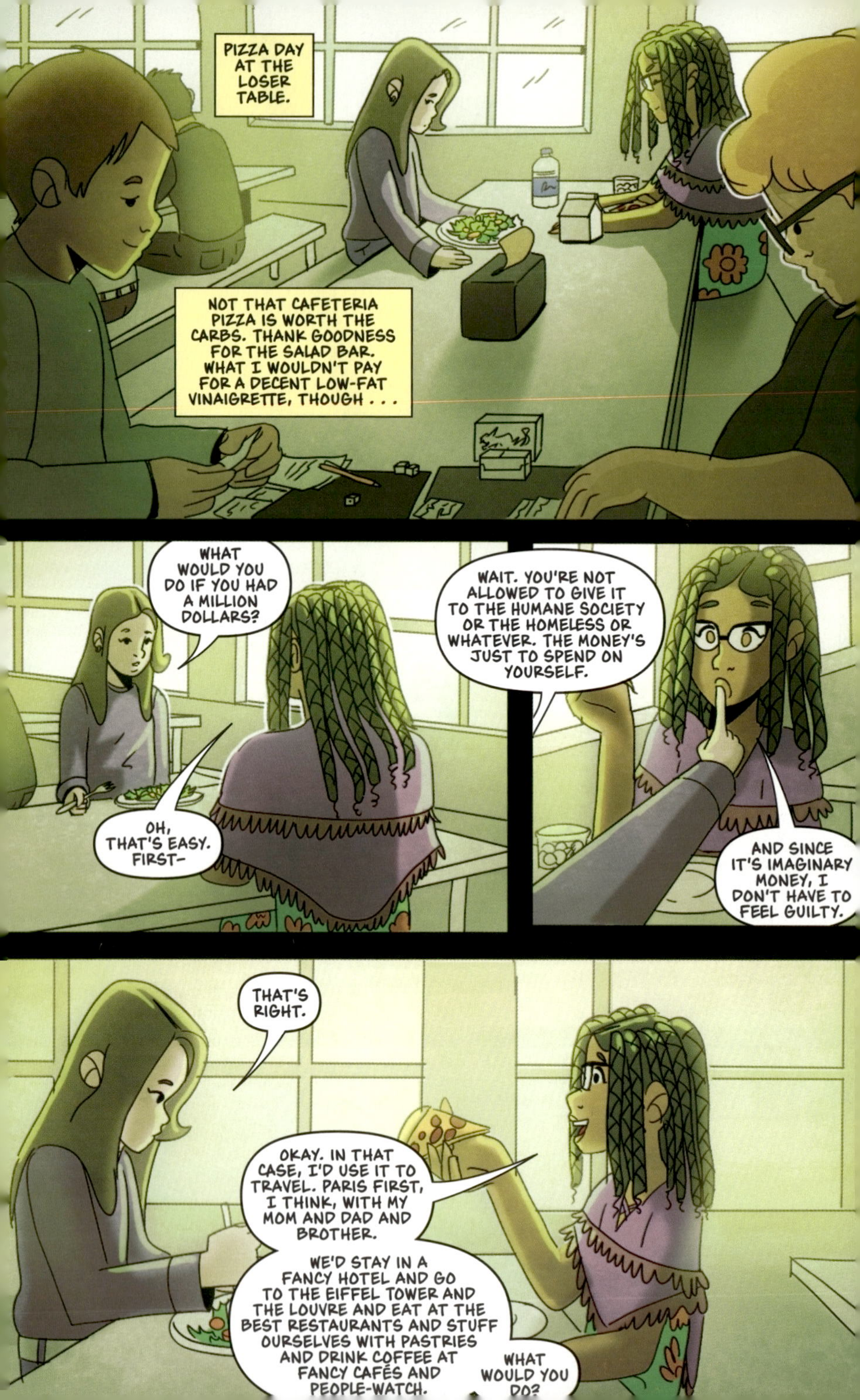
PIZZA DAY AT THE LOSER TABLE.
NOT THAT CAFETERIA PIZZA IS WORTH THE CARBS. THANK GOODNESS FOR THE SALAD BAR. WHAT I WOULDN'T PAY FOR A DECENT LOW-FAT VINAIGRETTE, THOUGH . . .
WHAT WOULD YOU DO IF YOU HAD A MILLION DOLLARS?
OH, THAT'S EASY. FIRST-
WAIT. YOU'RE NOT ALLOWED TO GIVE IT TO THE HUMANE SOCIETY OR THE HOMELESS OR WHATEVER. THE MONEY'S JUST TO SPEND ON YOURSELF.
AND SINCE IT'S IMAGINARY MONEY, I DON'T HAVE TO FEEL GUILTY.
THAT'S RIGHT.
OKAY. IN THAT CASE, I'D USE IT TO TRAVEL. PARIS FIRST, I THINK, WITH MY MOM AND DAD AND BROTHER.
WE'D STAY IN A FANCY HOTEL AND GO TO THE EIFFEL TOWER AND THE LOUVRE AND EAT AT THE BEST RESTAURANTS AND STUFF OURSELVES WITH PASTRIES AND DRINK COFFEE AT FANCY CAFÉS AND PEOPLE-WATCH.
WHAT WOULD YOU DO?

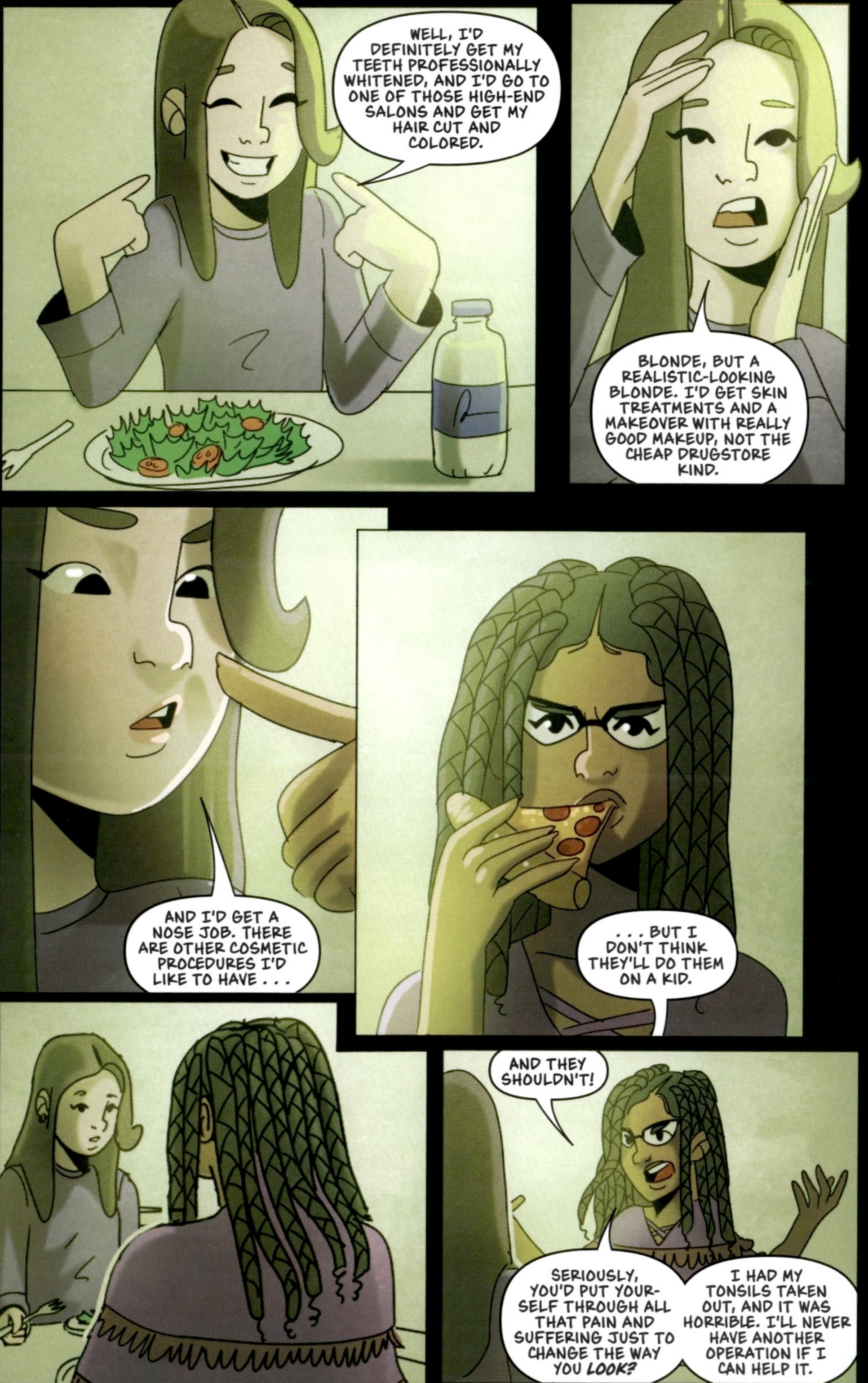

WELL, I'D DEFINITELY GET MY TEETH PROFESSIONALLY WHITENED, AND I'D GO TO ONE OF THOSE HIGH-END SALONS AND GET MY HAIR CUT AND COLORED.

BLONDE, BUT A REALISTIC-LOOKING BLONDE. I'D GET SKIN TREATMENTS AND A MAKEOVER WITH REALLY GOOD MAKEUP, NOT THE CHEAP DRUGSTORE KIND.

AND I'D GET A NOSE JOB. THERE ARE OTHER COSMETIC PROCEDURES I'D LIKE TO HAVE . . .

. . . BUT I DON'T THINK THEY'LL DO THEM ON A KID.

AND THEY SHOULDN'T!
SERIOUSLY, YOU'D PUT YOUR-SELF THROUGH ALL THAT PAIN AND SUFFERING JUST TO CHANGE THE WAY YOU *LOOK?*
I HAD MY TONSILS TAKEN OUT, AND IT WAS HORRIBLE. I'LL NEVER HAVE ANOTHER OPERATION IF I CAN HELP IT.

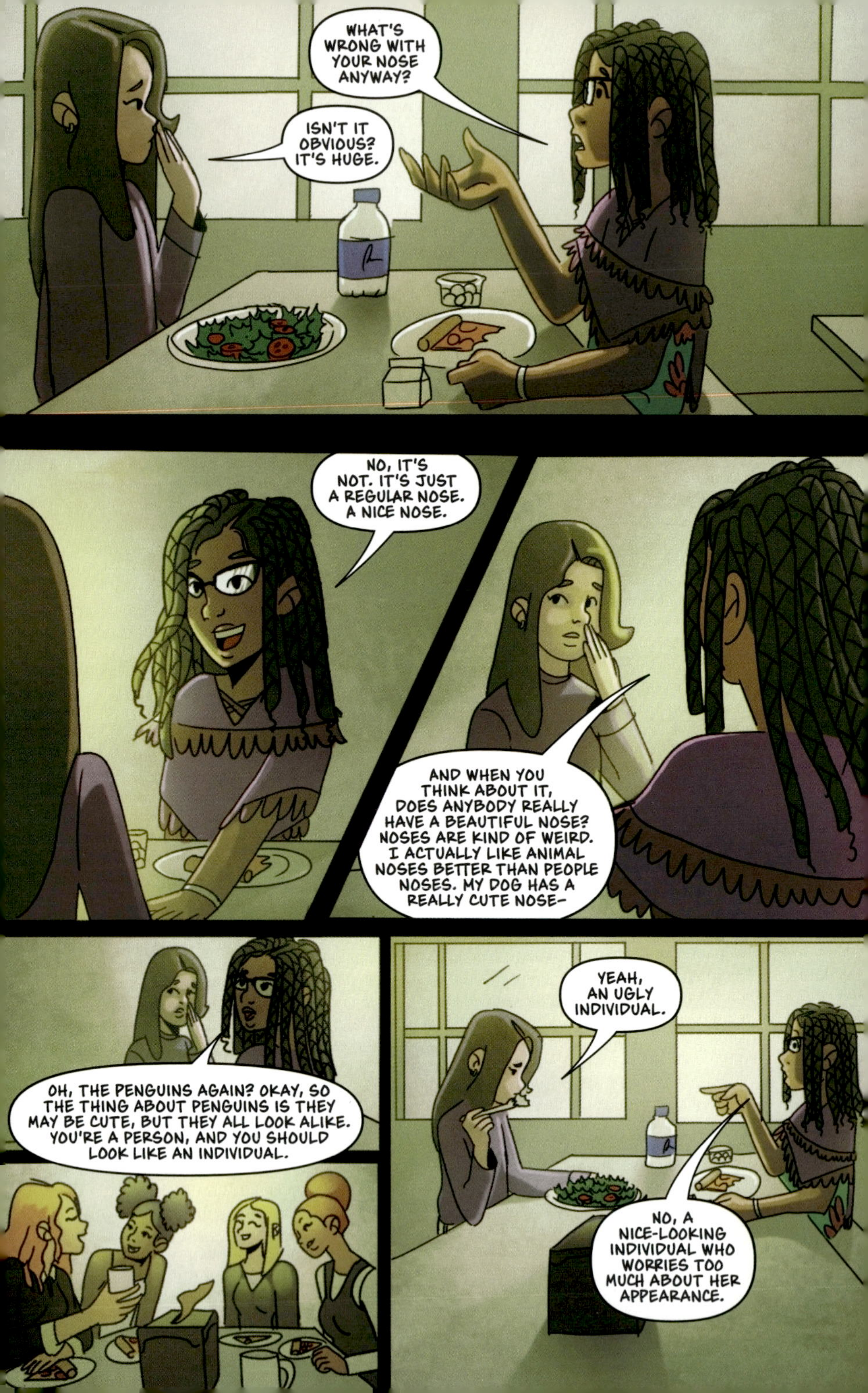

WHAT'S WRONG WITH YOUR NOSE ANYWAY?

ISN'T IT OBVIOUS? IT'S HUGE.

NO, IT'S NOT. IT'S JUST A REGULAR NOSE. A NICE NOSE.

AND WHEN YOU THINK ABOUT IT, DOES ANYBODY REALLY HAVE A BEAUTIFUL NOSE? NOSES ARE KIND OF WEIRD. I ACTUALLY LIKE ANIMAL NOSES BETTER THAN PEOPLE NOSES. MY DOG HAS A REALLY CUTE NOSE–

OH, THE PENGUINS AGAIN? OKAY, SO THE THING ABOUT PENGUINS IS THEY MAY BE CUTE, BUT THEY ALL LOOK ALIKE. YOU'RE A PERSON, AND YOU SHOULD LOOK LIKE AN INDIVIDUAL.

YEAH, AN UGLY INDIVIDUAL.

NO, A NICE-LOOKING INDIVIDUAL WHO WORRIES TOO MUCH ABOUT HER APPEARANCE.

YOU'VE CHANGED A LOT IN THE PAST COUPLE YEARS, SARAH. WE USED TO TALK ABOUT BOOKS AND MOVIES AND MUSIC.
NOW ALL YOU WANT TO TALK ABOUT IS HOW YOU DON'T LIKE THE WAY YOU LOOK AND ABOUT ALL THE CLOTHES AND HAIRSTYLES AND MAKEUP YOU WISH YOU COULD AFFORD.
HOW DARE SHE JUDGE ME?
FRIENDS ARE SUPPOSED TO BE THE PEOPLE WHO DON'T JUDGE YOU.
YOU'RE RIGHT, ABBY.
I HAVE CHANGED. I'VE GROWN UP, AND YOU HAVEN'T.
I THINK ABOUT ADULT THINGS, AND YOU STILL BUY STICKERS AND WATCH CARTOONS AND DRAW HORSES!
NO MORE HANGING OUT AT THE LOSER TABLE.
NO MORE ASKING MY MOM FOR PERMISSION TO BE BEAUTIFUL.
I'M GOING TO BE AS PRETTY AND AS POPULAR AS I CAN BE.

I DON'T NEED TO HAVE A MILLION DOLLARS TO BECOME A BLONDE.
I CAN DO IT FOR TEN BUCKS AND STILL LOOK LIKE A MILLION.
NOW, IF YOU WANT YOUR HAIR TO LOOK LIKE THE PICTURE, YOU'LL HAVE TO BLEACH IT FIRST.
LIKE THE STUFF MOM USES TO CLEAN THE FLOOR SOMETIMES? THAT CAN'T BE RIGHT.
HOW?
YOU'LL WANNA GET THE PEROXIDE OVER THERE.
DOES YOUR MAMA KNOW YOU'RE ABOUT TO COLOR YOUR HAIR, HON?
OH, SURE.
SHE'LL FIND OUT SOON ENOUGH.
WELL, THAT'S GOOD, THEN. MAYBE SHE CAN HELP YOU. MAKE SURE YOU GET THE COLOR ON GOOD AND EVEN.

MY SCALP IS BURNING.
THE STINK OF BLEACH MAKES MY EYES WATER.
AND NOW I LOOK LIKE AN OLD WOMAN.
BUT IT WILL ALL BE WORTH IT SOON.
TIME TO COMPLETE THE TRANSFORMATION. AND ALL BEFORE MOM CAN EVEN GET HOME.

SOON . . .
SARAH, I'M HOME–
AAAAAAAAAAAAAAAAAAA!!!
SARAH?!
I–I WANTED TO BE BLONDE, BUT I'M–I'M . . .
GREEN. I CAN SEE THAT.
PUT ON YOUR SHOES.

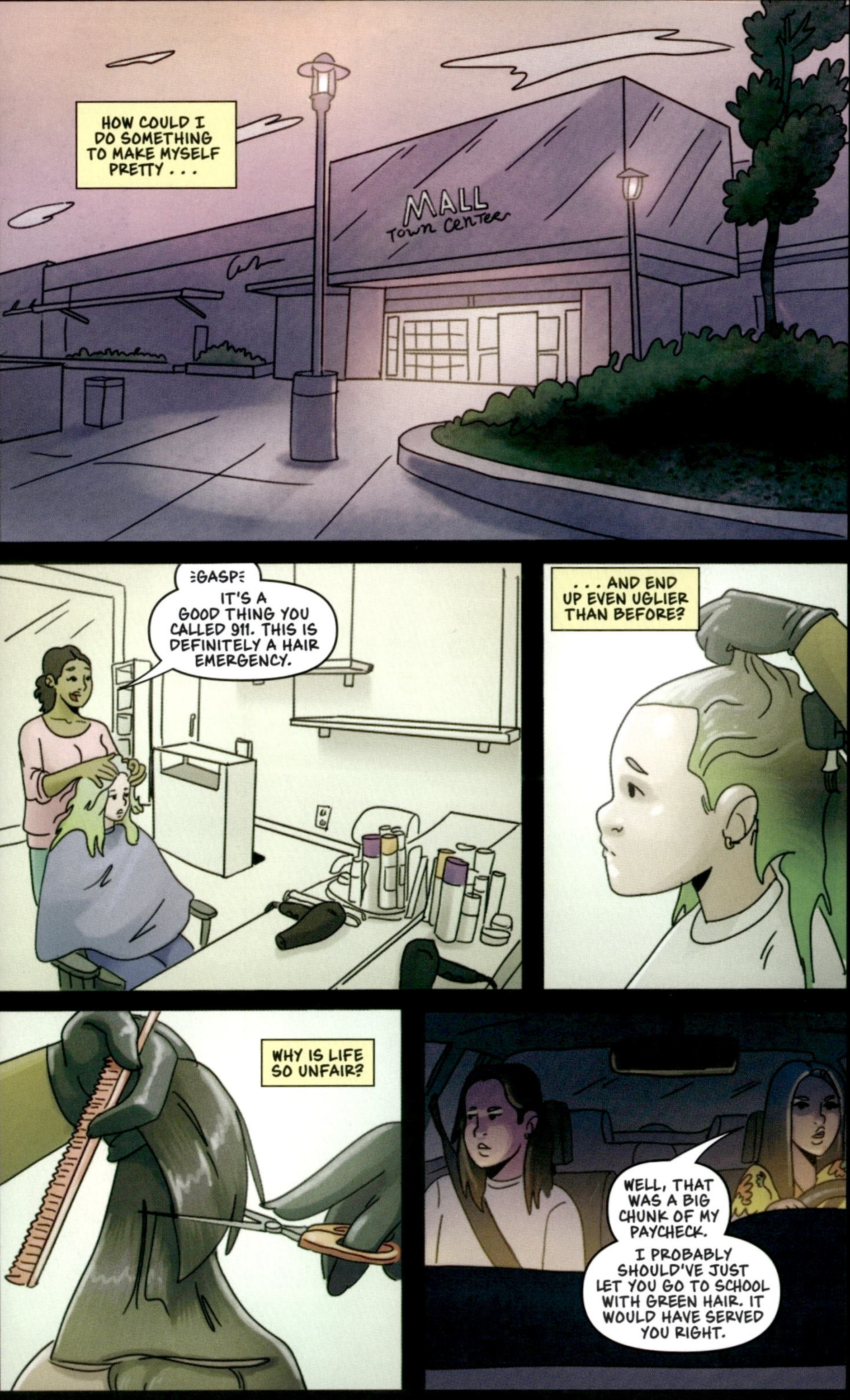

HOW COULD I DO SOMETHING TO MAKE MYSELF PRETTY . . .

MALL
Town Center

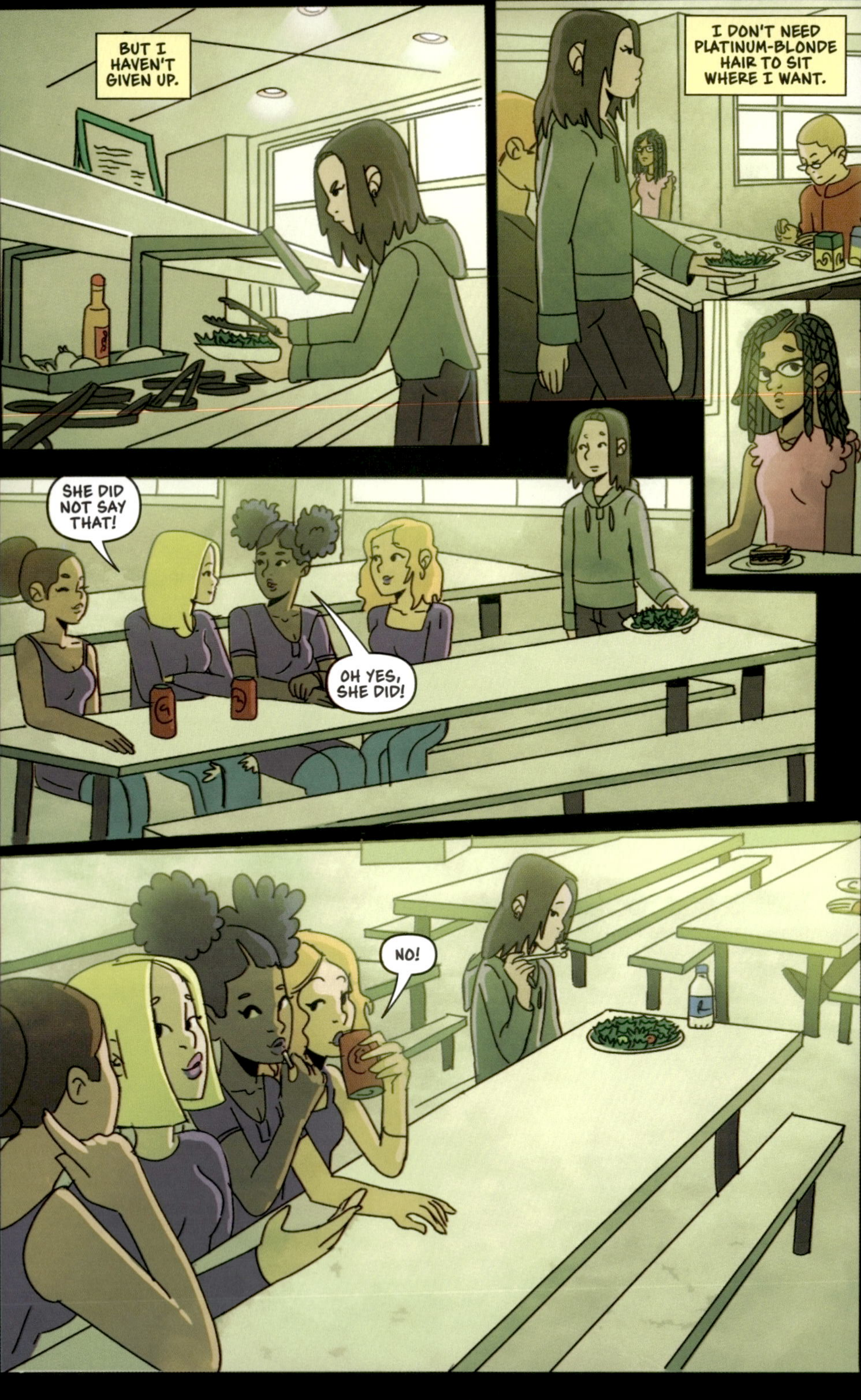
BUT I HAVEN'T GIVEN UP.
I DON'T NEED PLATINUM-BLONDE HAIR TO SIT WHERE I WANT.
SHE DID NOT SAY THAT!
OH YES, SHE DID!
NO!

YES!
WHO ARE THEY TALKING ABOUT?

AND THEN WHAT DID HE SAY?
I CAN'T FOLLOW ANY OF THIS.

I'M CERTAINLY NOT GOING TO ASK THEM. IF THEY CAN'T SEE ME, THEY WOULDN'T BE ABLE TO HEAR ME, EITHER.
IT'S LIKE I'M A GHOST.
I CAN'T. I CAN'T DO THIS. I HAVE TO-

WHACK
MASON BLAIR, THE MOST PERFECT GUY IN SCHOOL-
WATCH WHERE YOU'RE GOING.

SORRY!

WHAT A NIGHTMARE. I NEVER WANTED MASON TO NOTICE ME LIKE THIS. NOT AS AN UGLY, CLUMSY GIRL WITH FRIED, FRIZZY BROWN HAIR WHO GAVE A NEW MEANING TO THE WORDS "TOSSED SALAD."

WHY DOES EVERYTHING HAVE TO GO WRONG FOR ME?
RIIIIIIING

THE BEAUTIFULS NEVER DO ANYTHING STUPID OR CLUMSY OR HUMILIATING IN FRONT OF A CUTE BOY.
THEIR BEAUTY IS LIKE A SUIT OF ARMOR.
AND OF COURSE THEY CAN SCARF ALL THE ICE CREAM THEY WANT AND NOT GAIN AN OUNCE.
ICE
IT'S ALL SO UNFAIR.

JU
J
I'M SURE NONE OF THE BEAUTIFULS HAVE TO PASS A PLACE SO HIDEOUS ON THEIR WAY HOME . . .
IS THERE A PERSON TRAPPED IN THERE?

METAL . . .
BUT WHAT IS IT? SOME KIND OF DOLL?
NO WAY THE TRUNK WILL OPEN PROPERLY IN THIS RUSTED, DENTED UP WRECK.
JUST LIKE *THE SWORD IN THE STONE*. CAN I PULL WHATEVER THIS IS OUT?
GASP!
WHO WOULD THROW THIS OUT?

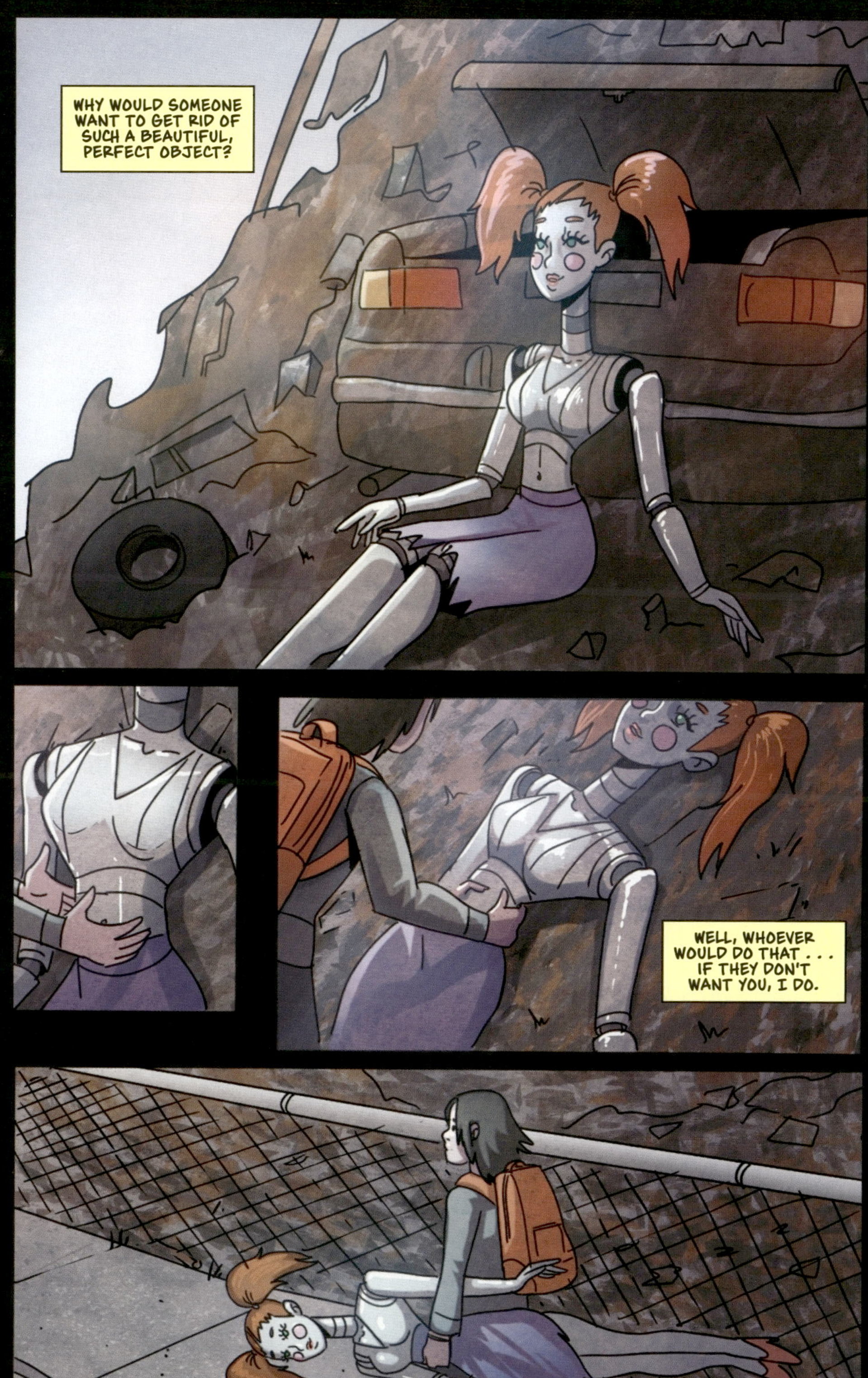
WHY WOULD SOMEONE WANT TO GET RID OF SUCH A BEAUTIFUL, PERFECT OBJECT?
WELL, WHOEVER WOULD DO THAT . . . IF THEY DON'T WANT YOU, I DO.

THERE. WELCOME HOME.
COULD USE A LITTLE MORE CARE, THOUGH . . .
THAT'S BETTER-
CLIK
VVVVVVVRRRRRMMMMM
WHAT DID I DO?
CLIK RRrrrRRR CHKNTK CHKNTK
VVVRRRRRRMMMMMmmmmmm...
IS IT GOING TO BLOW UP?!

HELLO, FRIEND.
H-HI?
MY NAME IS ELEANOR.
I'M SARAH.
NICE TO MEET YOU, SARAH.
WHOA. THERE MUST BE SOME PRETTY SOPHISTICATED COMPUTER IN THERE OR SOMETHING, TO SAY MY NAME BACK TO ME . . .
THANK YOU FOR RESCUING ME AND CLEANING ME UP, SARAH.
I FEEL AS GOOD AS NEW.
IS THIS THING CAPABLE OF ACTUAL CONVERSATION? ACTUAL THOUGHT?
YOU'RE WELCOME?
NOW, YOU TELL ME WHAT I CAN DO FOR YOU, SARAH.

WHAT DO YOU MEAN?
YOU DID SOMETHING NICE FOR ME. NOW I MUST DO SOMETHING NICE FOR YOU.
A ROBOT CAN'T JUST MAKE WISHES COME TRUE.
WHAT DO YOU WANT, SARAH? I WANT TO MAKE YOUR WISHES COME TRUE.
UH, NOTHING, REALLY . . .
EVERYBODY WANTS SOMETHING.
WHAT DO YOU WANT, SARAH?
I MIGHT AS WELL SAY IT. ELEANOR'S A ROBOT. AT LEAST SHE WON'T JUDGE ME.
I WANT . . .
I WANT TO BE BEAUTIFUL.

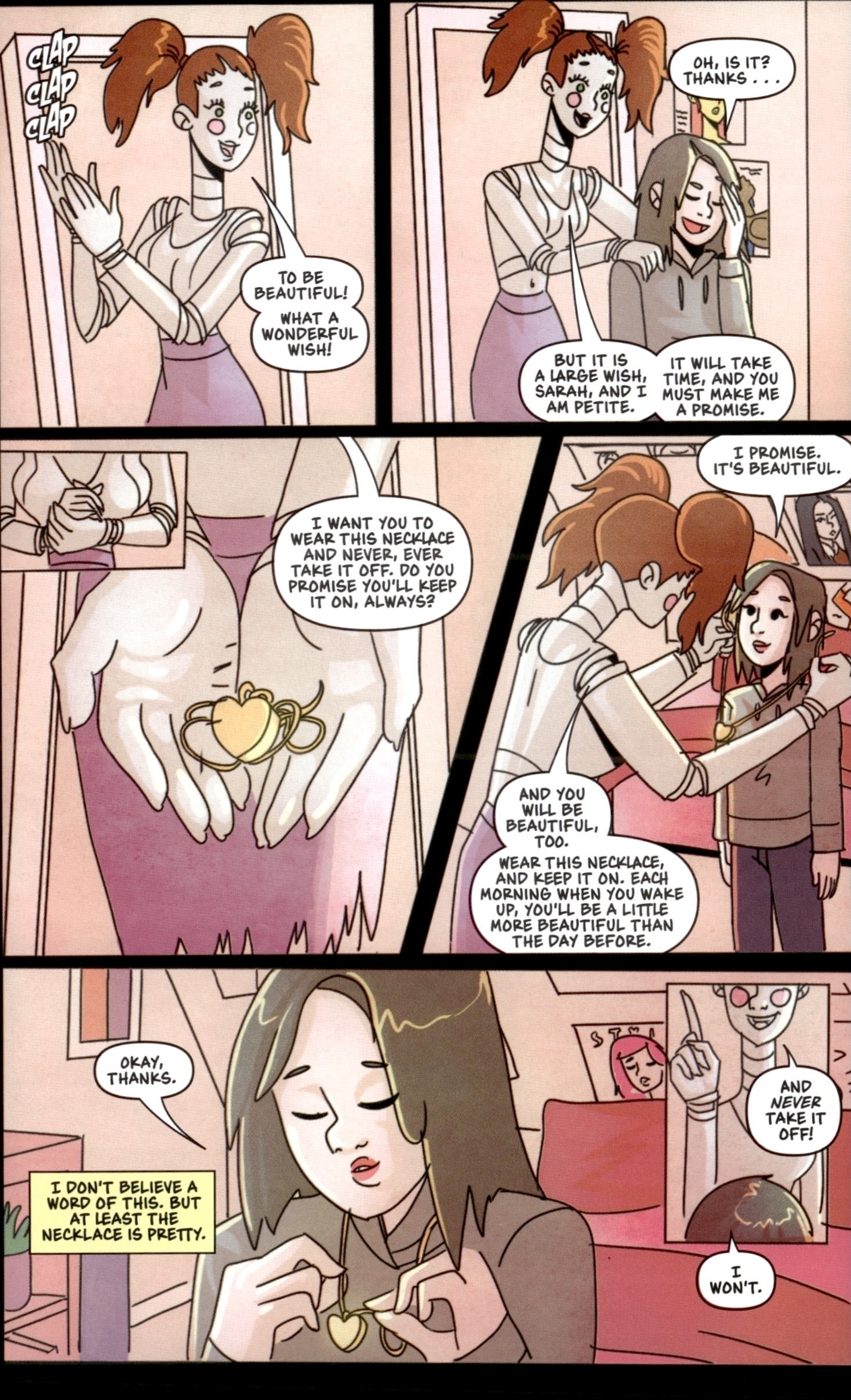
CLAP
CLAP
CLAP
TO BE BEAUTIFUL!
WHAT A WONDERFUL WISH!
OH, IS IT? THANKS . . .
BUT IT IS A LARGE WISH, SARAH, AND I AM PETITE.
IT WILL TAKE TIME, AND YOU MUST MAKE ME A PROMISE.
I WANT YOU TO WEAR THIS NECKLACE AND NEVER, EVER TAKE IT OFF. DO YOU PROMISE YOU'LL KEEP IT ON, ALWAYS?
I PROMISE. IT'S BEAUTIFUL.
AND YOU WILL BE BEAUTIFUL, TOO.
WEAR THIS NECKLACE, AND KEEP IT ON. EACH MORNING WHEN YOU WAKE UP, YOU'LL BE A LITTLE MORE BEAUTIFUL THAN THE DAY BEFORE.
OKAY, THANKS.
I DON'T BELIEVE A WORD OF THIS. BUT AT LEAST THE NECKLACE IS PRETTY.
AND NEVER TAKE IT OFF!
I WON'T.

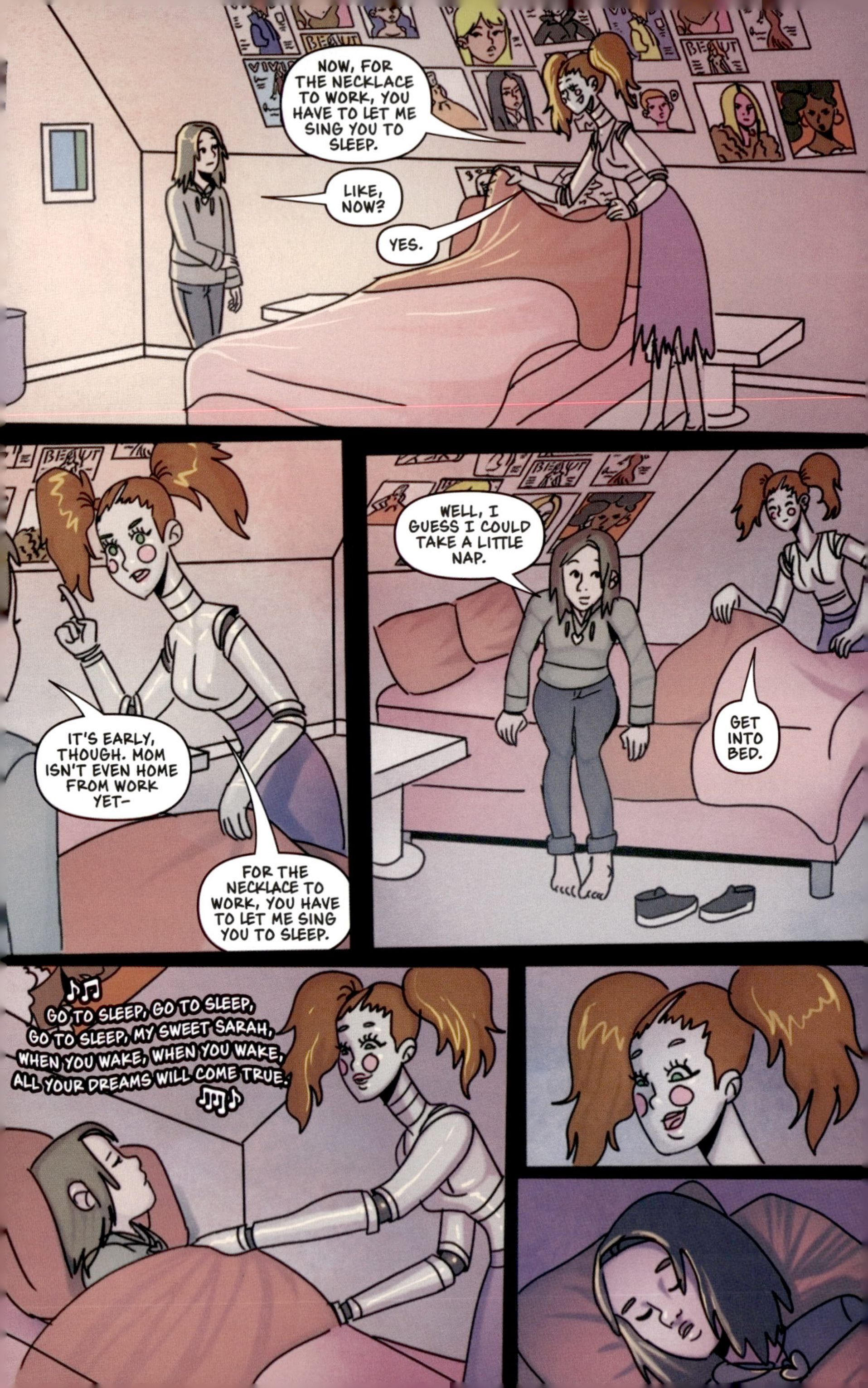
NOW, FOR THE NECKLACE TO WORK, YOU HAVE TO LET ME SING YOU TO SLEEP.
LIKE, NOW?
YES.
IT'S EARLY, THOUGH. MOM ISN'T EVEN HOME FROM WORK YET-
FOR THE NECKLACE TO WORK, YOU HAVE TO LET ME SING YOU TO SLEEP.
WELL, I GUESS I COULD TAKE A LITTLE NAP.
GET INTO BED.
GO TO SLEEP, GO TO SLEEP, GO TO SLEEP, MY SWEET SARAH, WHEN YOU WAKE, WHEN YOU WAKE, ALL YOUR DREAMS WILL COME TRUE.

THE NEXT MORNING . . .
DID I SLEEP ALL NIGHT?
I FEEL SO MUCH BETTER THAN MOST MORNINGS. I MUST HAVE REALLY NEEDED IT.
DID I DREAM THAT STUFF WITH THE ROBOT-
NO, REAL.
WAIT, WHAT'S UP WITH MY . . .
MY HANDS! MY ARMS!
ELEANOR! DID YOU . . . ?

MY ARMS, MY HANDS, EVEN MY FINGERS! THEY'RE BEAUTIFUL!
EVEN THE SKIN IS SOFTER!
SAME MIX-AND-MATCH FACE, NOSE, AND BODY, BUT . . .
"EACH MORNING WHEN YOU WAKE UP, YOU'LL BE A LITTLE MORE BEAUTIFUL THAN THE DAY BEFORE."
I LOVE MY NEW ARMS AND HANDS! THANK YOU!
SO, LIKE, AM I GOING TO WAKE UP EVERY MORNING TO ONE NEW PART UNTIL I'M TOTALLY TRANSFORMED?
. . .
I'LL JUST HAVE TO WAIT AND SEE, HUH?
THANKS AGAIN.

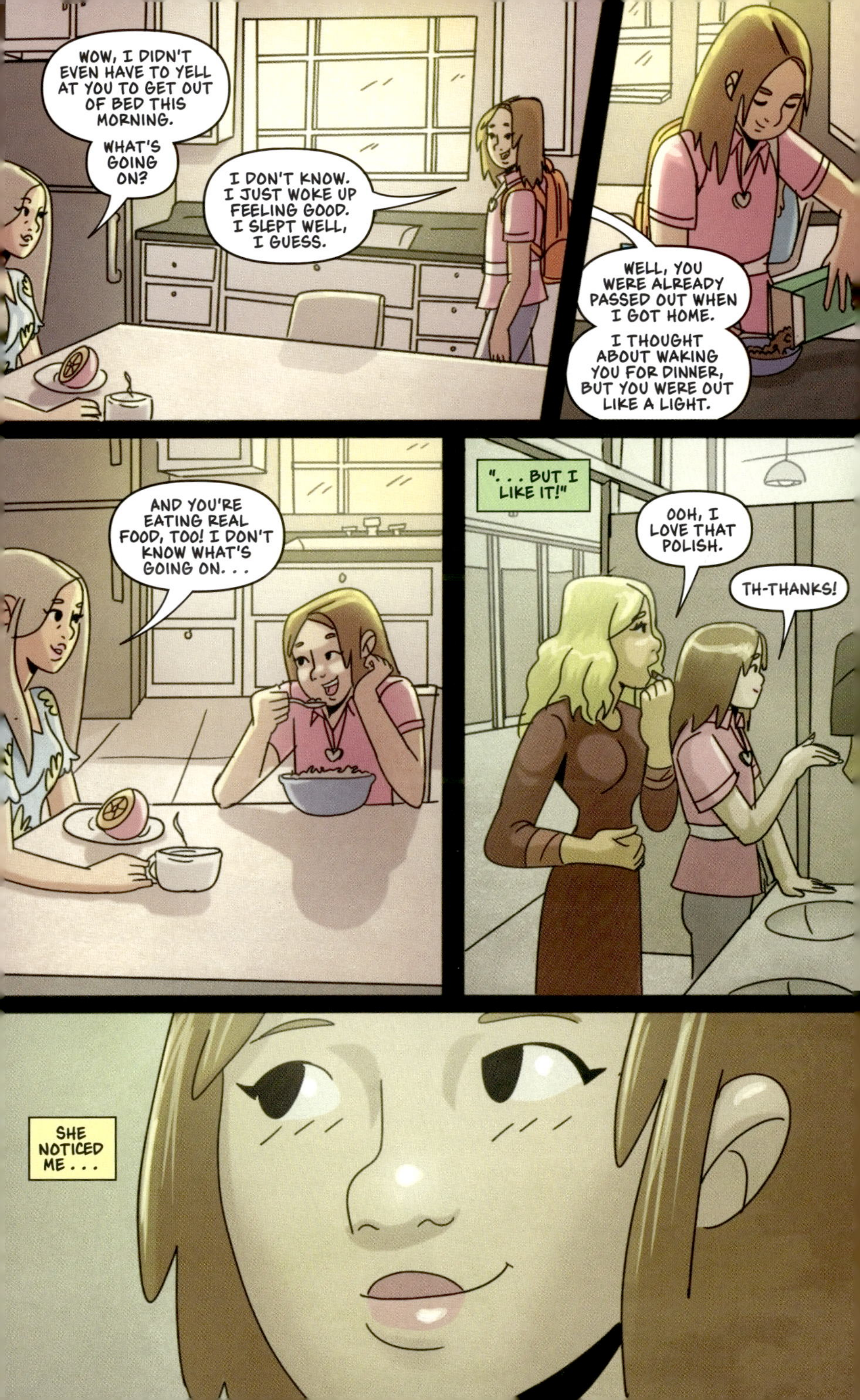
WOW, I DIDN'T EVEN HAVE TO YELL AT YOU TO GET OUT OF BED THIS MORNING.
WHAT'S GOING ON?
I DON'T KNOW. I JUST WOKE UP FEELING GOOD. I SLEPT WELL, I GUESS.
WELL, YOU WERE ALREADY PASSED OUT WHEN I GOT HOME.
I THOUGHT ABOUT WAKING YOU FOR DINNER, BUT YOU WERE OUT LIKE A LIGHT.
AND YOU'RE EATING REAL FOOD, TOO! I DON'T KNOW WHAT'S GOING ON. . .
". . . BUT I LIKE IT!"
OOH, I LOVE THAT POLISH.
TH-THANKS!
SHE NOTICED ME . . .

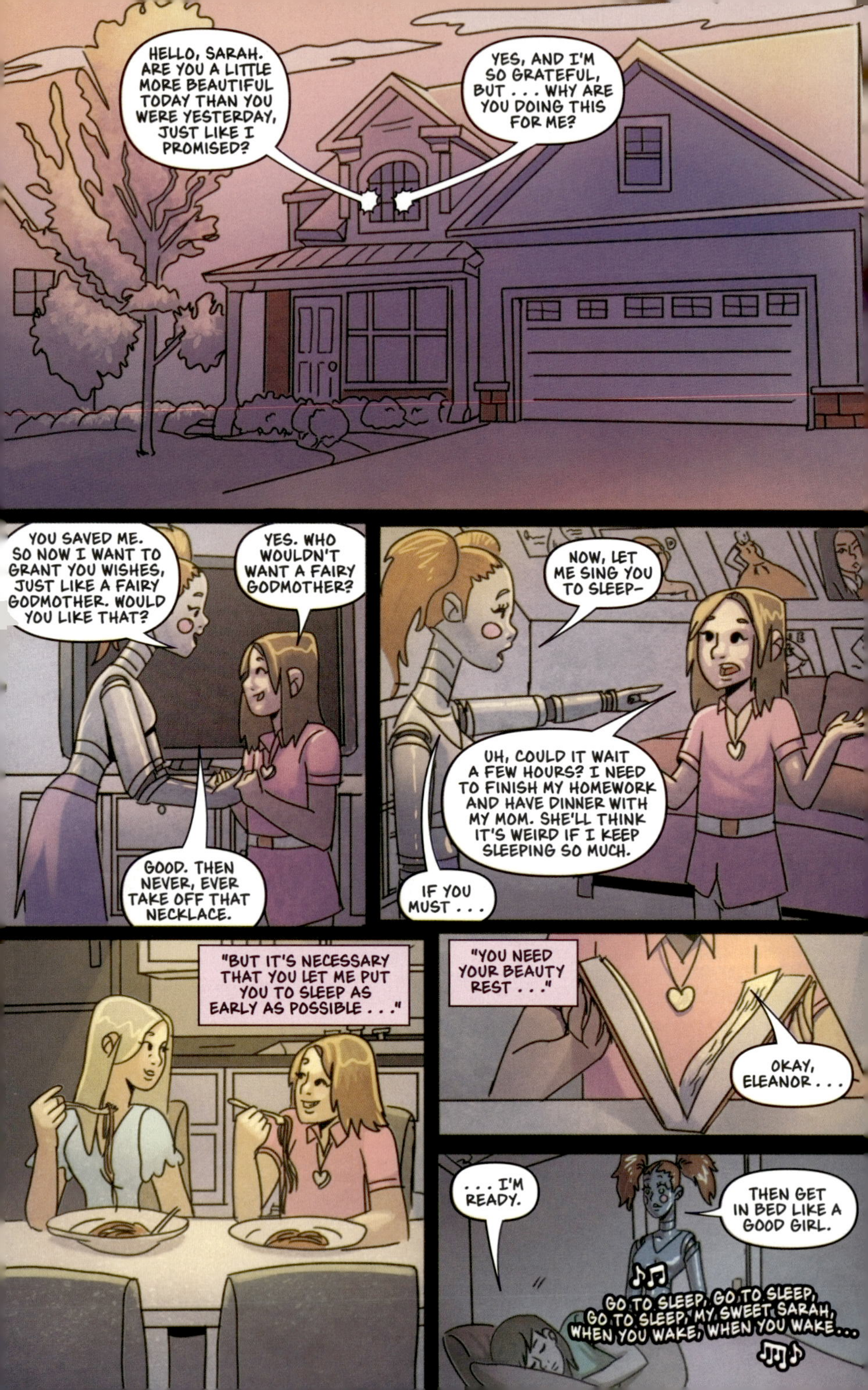
HELLO, SARAH. ARE YOU A LITTLE MORE BEAUTIFUL TODAY THAN YOU WERE YESTERDAY, JUST LIKE I PROMISED?
YES, AND I'M SO GRATEFUL, BUT . . . WHY ARE YOU DOING THIS FOR ME?
YOU SAVED ME. SO NOW I WANT TO GRANT YOU WISHES, JUST LIKE A FAIRY GODMOTHER. WOULD YOU LIKE THAT?
YES. WHO WOULDN'T WANT A FAIRY GODMOTHER?
GOOD. THEN NEVER, EVER TAKE OFF THAT NECKLACE.
NOW, LET ME SING YOU TO SLEEP-
UH, COULD IT WAIT A FEW HOURS? I NEED TO FINISH MY HOMEWORK AND HAVE DINNER WITH MY MOM. SHE'LL THINK IT'S WEIRD IF I KEEP SLEEPING SO MUCH.
IF YOU MUST . . .
"BUT IT'S NECESSARY THAT YOU LET ME PUT YOU TO SLEEP AS EARLY AS POSSIBLE . . ."
"YOU NEED YOUR BEAUTY REST . . ."
OKAY, ELEANOR . . .
. . . I'M READY.
THEN GET IN BED LIKE A GOOD GIRL.
GO TO SLEEP, GO TO SLEEP, GO TO SLEEP, MY SWEET SARAH, WHEN YOU WAKE, WHEN YOU WAKE . . .

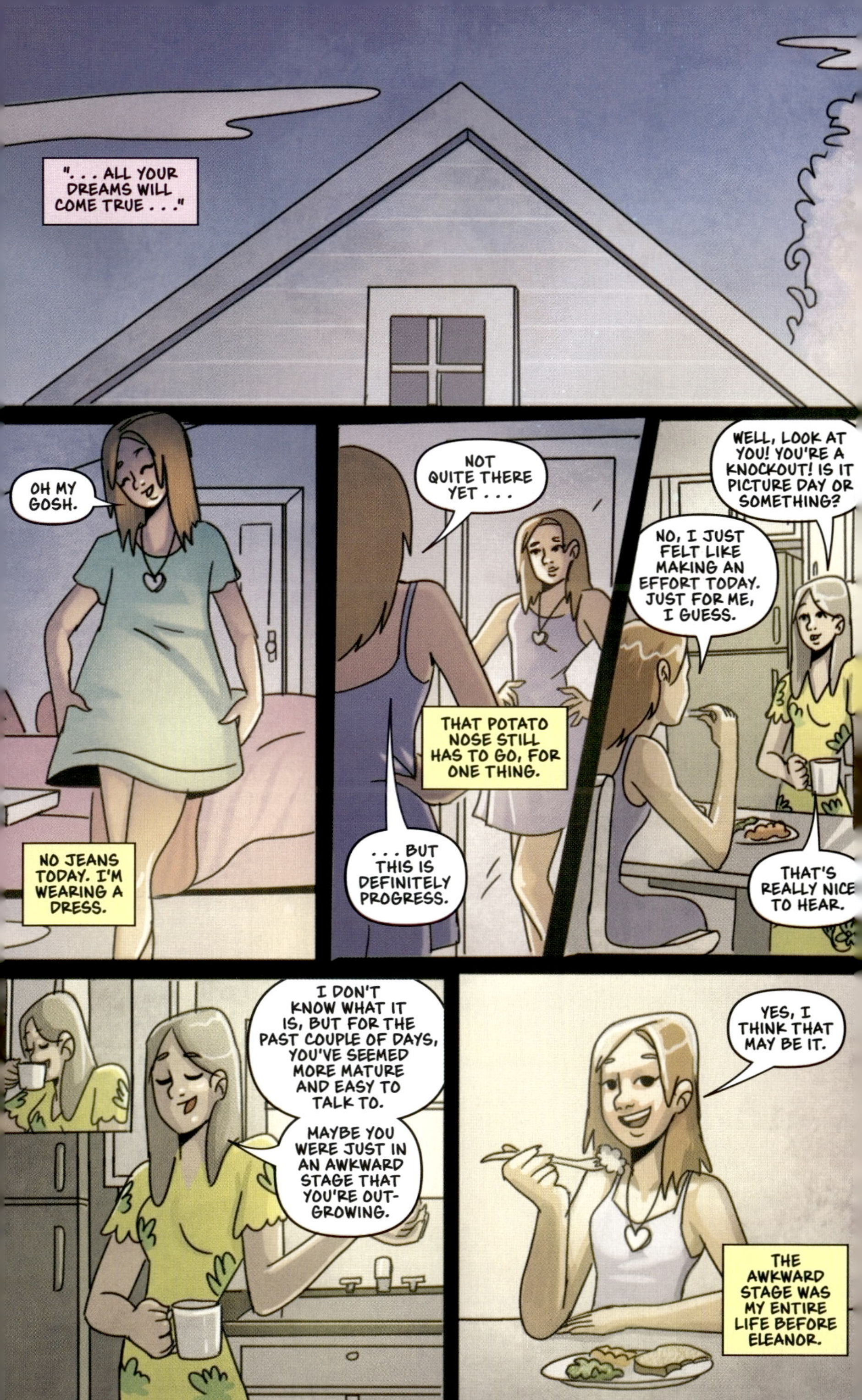
". . . ALL YOUR DREAMS WILL COME TRUE . . ."
OH MY GOSH.
NO JEANS TODAY. I'M WEARING A DRESS.
NOT QUITE THERE YET . . .
THAT POTATO NOSE STILL HAS TO GO, FOR ONE THING.
. . . BUT THIS IS DEFINITELY PROGRESS.
WELL, LOOK AT YOU! YOU'RE A KNOCKOUT! IS IT PICTURE DAY OR SOMETHING?
NO, I JUST FELT LIKE MAKING AN EFFORT TODAY. JUST FOR ME, I GUESS.
THAT'S REALLY NICE TO HEAR.
I DON'T KNOW WHAT IT IS, BUT FOR THE PAST COUPLE OF DAYS, YOU'VE SEEMED MORE MATURE AND EASY TO TALK TO.
MAYBE YOU WERE JUST IN AN AWKWARD STAGE THAT YOU'RE OUT-GROWING.
YES, I THINK THAT MAY BE IT.
THE AWKWARD STAGE WAS MY ENTIRE LIFE BEFORE ELEANOR.

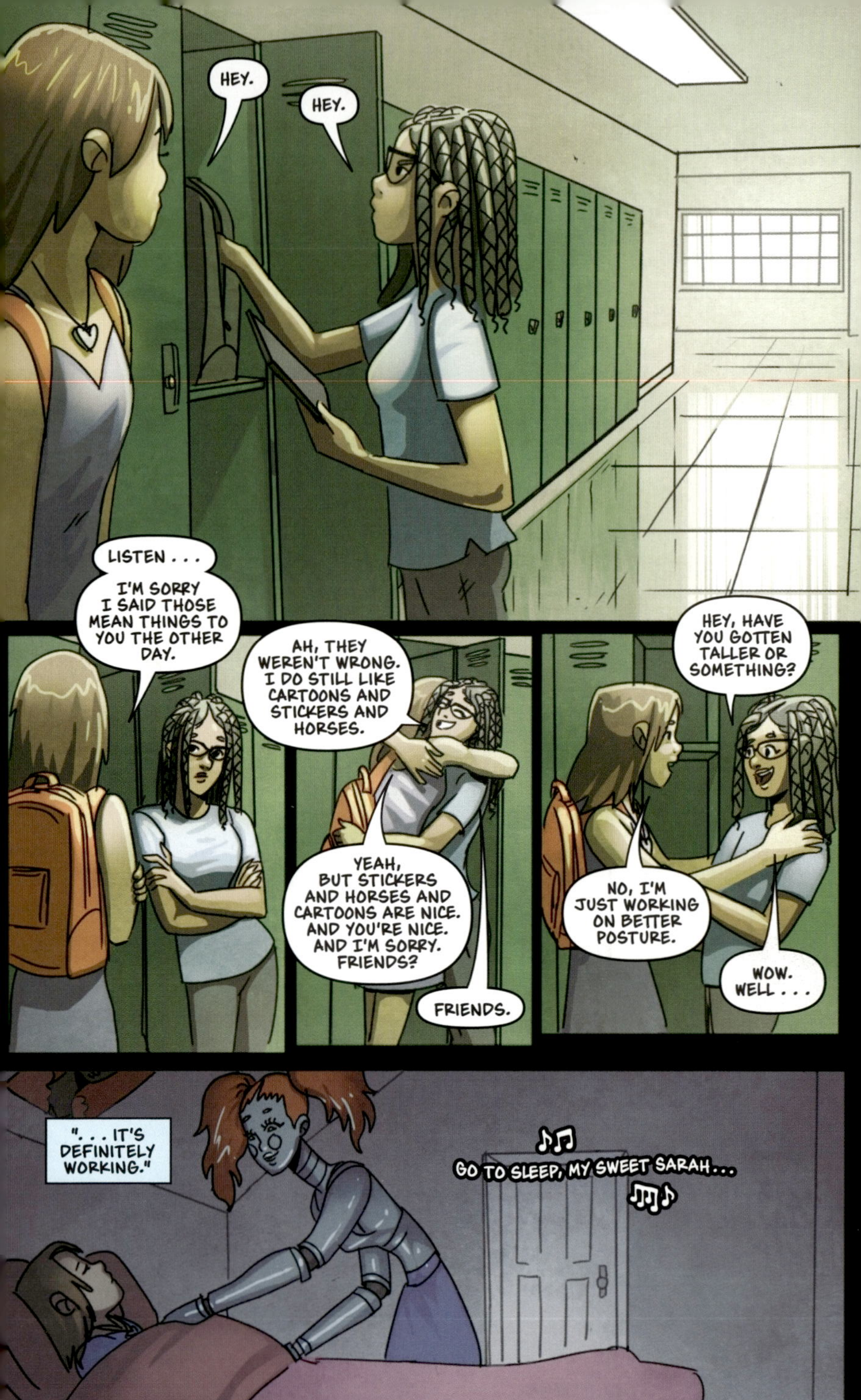
HEY.
HEY.
LISTEN . . .
I'M SORRY I SAID THOSE MEAN THINGS TO YOU THE OTHER DAY.
AH, THEY WEREN'T WRONG. I DO STILL LIKE CARTOONS AND STICKERS AND HORSES.
YEAH, BUT STICKERS AND HORSES AND CARTOONS ARE NICE. AND YOU'RE NICE. AND I'M SORRY. FRIENDS?
FRIENDS.
HEY, HAVE YOU GOTTEN TALLER OR SOMETHING?
NO, I'M JUST WORKING ON BETTER POSTURE.
WOW. WELL . . .
". . . IT'S DEFINITELY WORKING."
GO TO SLEEP, MY SWEET SARAH . . .

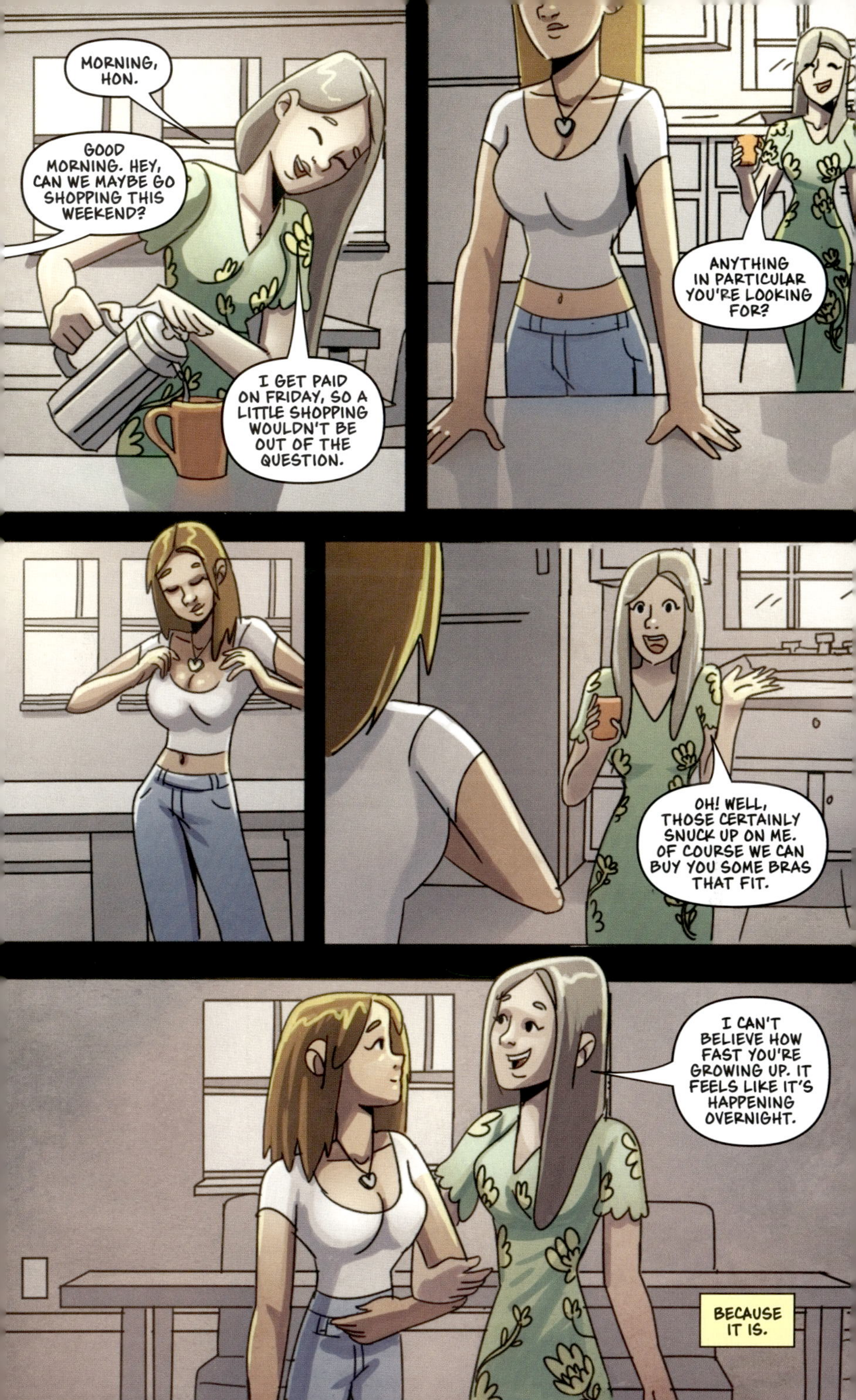
MORNING, HON.
GOOD MORNING. HEY, CAN WE MAYBE GO SHOPPING THIS WEEKEND?
I GET PAID ON FRIDAY, SO A LITTLE SHOPPING WOULDN'T BE OUT OF THE QUESTION.
ANYTHING IN PARTICULAR YOU'RE LOOKING FOR?
OH! WELL, THOSE CERTAINLY SNUCK UP ON ME. OF COURSE WE CAN BUY YOU SOME BRAS THAT FIT.
I CAN'T BELIEVE HOW FAST YOU'RE GROWING UP. IT FEELS LIKE IT'S HAPPENING OVERNIGHT.
BECAUSE IT IS.

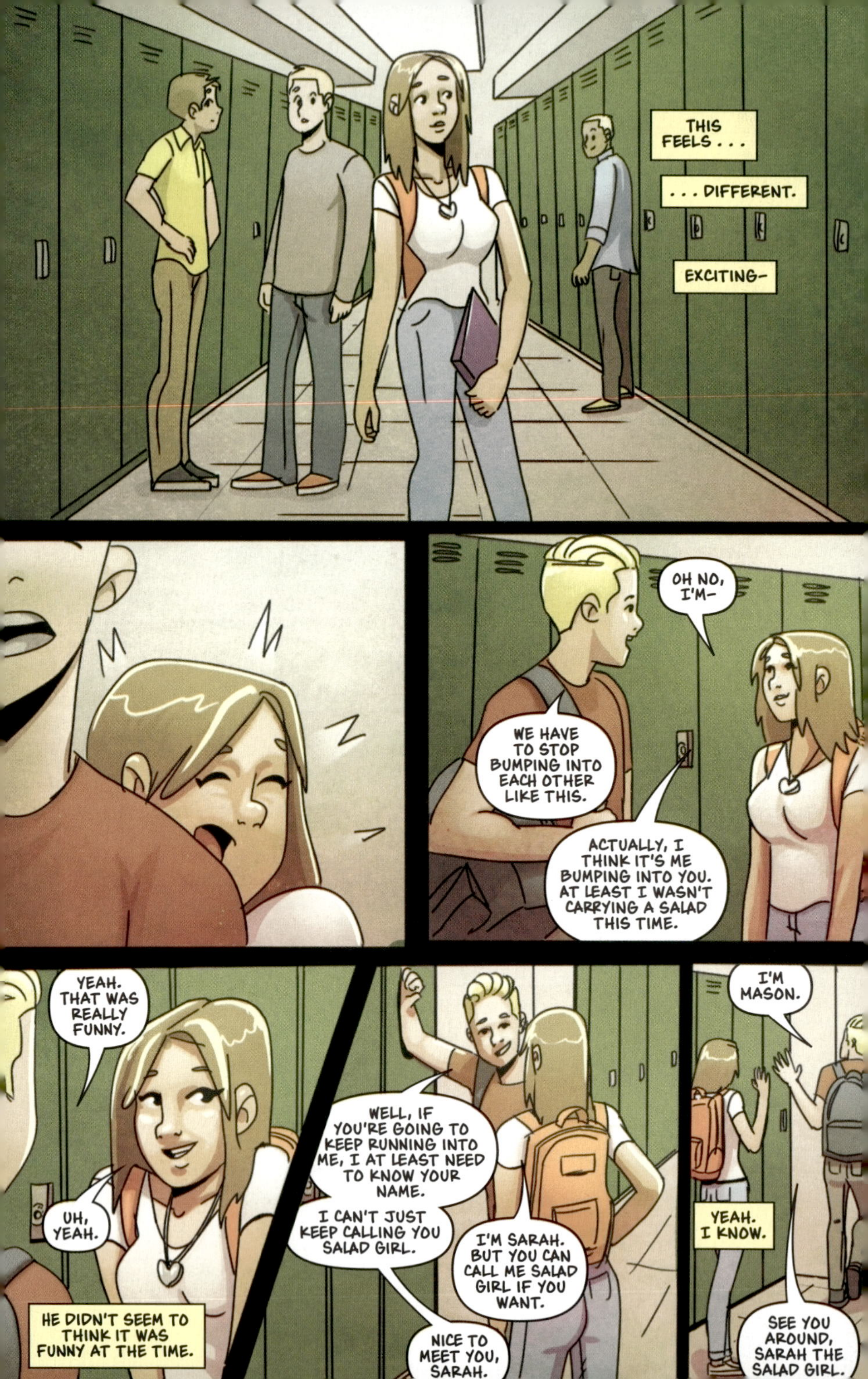
THIS FEELS . . .
. . . DIFFERENT.
EXCITING-
OH NO, I'M-
WE HAVE TO STOP BUMPING INTO EACH OTHER LIKE THIS.
ACTUALLY, I THINK IT'S ME BUMPING INTO YOU. AT LEAST I WASN'T CARRYING A SALAD THIS TIME.
YEAH. THAT WAS REALLY FUNNY.
UH, YEAH.
HE DIDN'T SEEM TO THINK IT WAS FUNNY AT THE TIME.
WELL, IF YOU'RE GOING TO KEEP RUNNING INTO ME, I AT LEAST NEED TO KNOW YOUR NAME.
I CAN'T JUST KEEP CALLING YOU SALAD GIRL.
I'M SARAH. BUT YOU CAN CALL ME SALAD GIRL IF YOU WANT.
NICE TO MEET YOU, SARAH.
I'M MASON.
YEAH. I KNOW.
SEE YOU AROUND, SARAH THE SALAD GIRL.

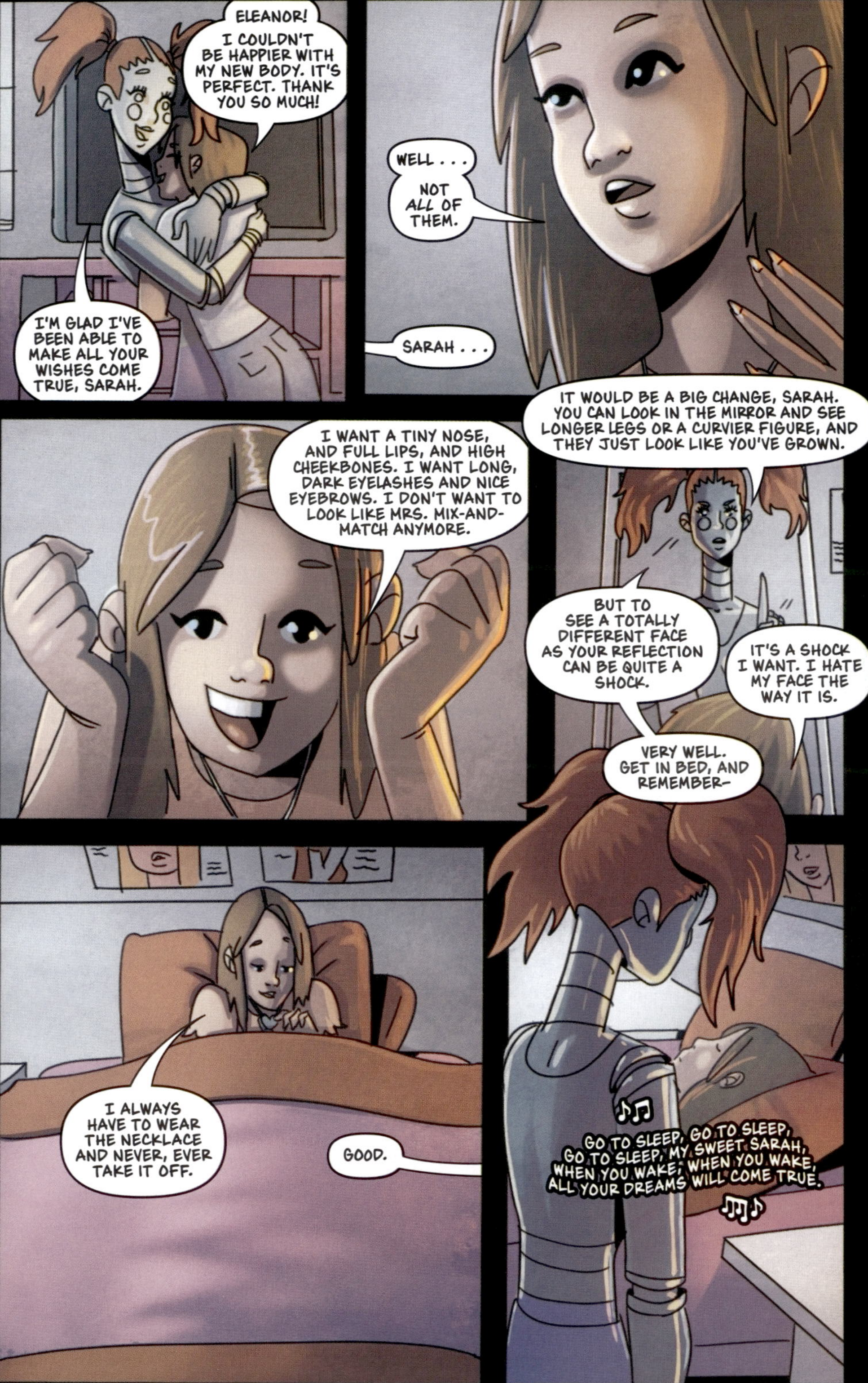
ELEANOR!
I COULDN'T BE HAPPIER WITH MY NEW BODY. IT'S PERFECT. THANK YOU SO MUCH!
I'M GLAD I'VE BEEN ABLE TO MAKE ALL YOUR WISHES COME TRUE, SARAH.
WELL . . .
NOT ALL OF THEM.
SARAH . . .
I WANT A TINY NOSE, AND FULL LIPS, AND HIGH CHEEKBONES. I WANT LONG, DARK EYELASHES AND NICE EYEBROWS. I DON'T WANT TO LOOK LIKE MRS. MIX-AND-MATCH ANYMORE.
IT WOULD BE A BIG CHANGE, SARAH. YOU CAN LOOK IN THE MIRROR AND SEE LONGER LEGS OR A CURVIER FIGURE, AND THEY JUST LOOK LIKE YOU'VE GROWN.
BUT TO SEE A TOTALLY DIFFERENT FACE AS YOUR REFLECTION CAN BE QUITE A SHOCK.
IT'S A SHOCK I WANT. I HATE MY FACE THE WAY IT IS.
VERY WELL. GET IN BED, AND REMEMBER-
I ALWAYS HAVE TO WEAR THE NECKLACE AND NEVER, EVER TAKE IT OFF.
GOOD.
GO TO SLEEP, GO TO SLEEP, GO TO SLEEP, MY SWEET SARAH, WHEN YOU WAKE, WHEN YOU WAKE, ALL YOUR DREAMS WILL COME TRUE.

IT'S MORNING! DID IT-
IT WORKED.

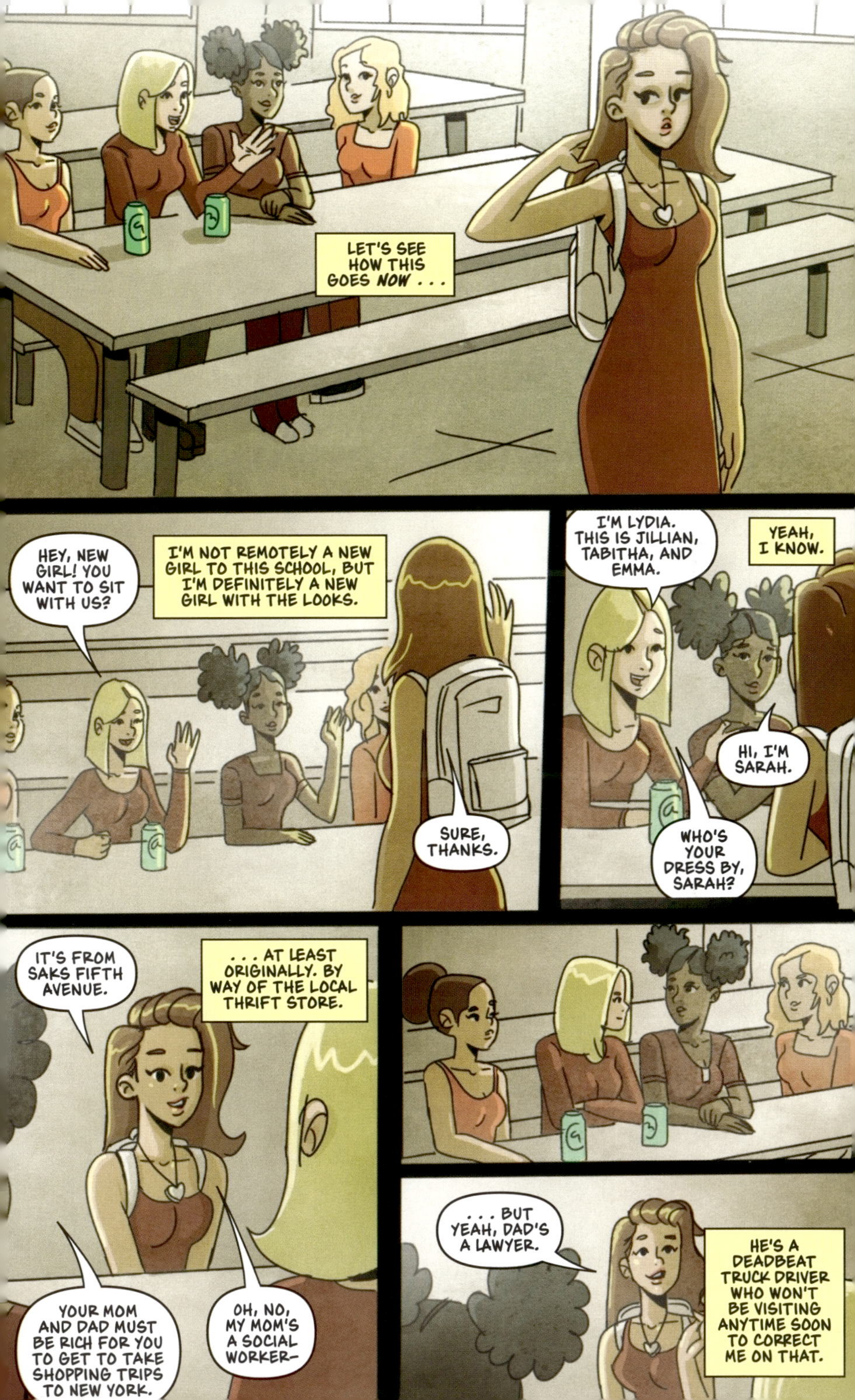
LET'S SEE HOW THIS GOES NOW . . .
HEY, NEW GIRL! YOU WANT TO SIT WITH US?
I'M NOT REMOTELY A NEW GIRL TO THIS SCHOOL, BUT I'M DEFINITELY A NEW GIRL WITH THE LOOKS.
SURE, THANKS.
I'M LYDIA. THIS IS JILLIAN, TABITHA, AND EMMA.
YEAH, I KNOW.
HI, I'M SARAH.
WHO'S YOUR DRESS BY, SARAH?
IT'S FROM SAKS FIFTH AVENUE.
. . . AT LEAST ORIGINALLY. BY WAY OF THE LOCAL THRIFT STORE.
YOUR MOM AND DAD MUST BE RICH FOR YOU TO GET TO TAKE SHOPPING TRIPS TO NEW YORK.
OH, NO, MY MOM'S A SOCIAL WORKER–
. . . BUT YEAH, DAD'S A LAWYER.
HE'S A DEADBEAT TRUCK DRIVER WHO WON'T BE VISITING ANYTIME SOON TO CORRECT ME ON THAT.

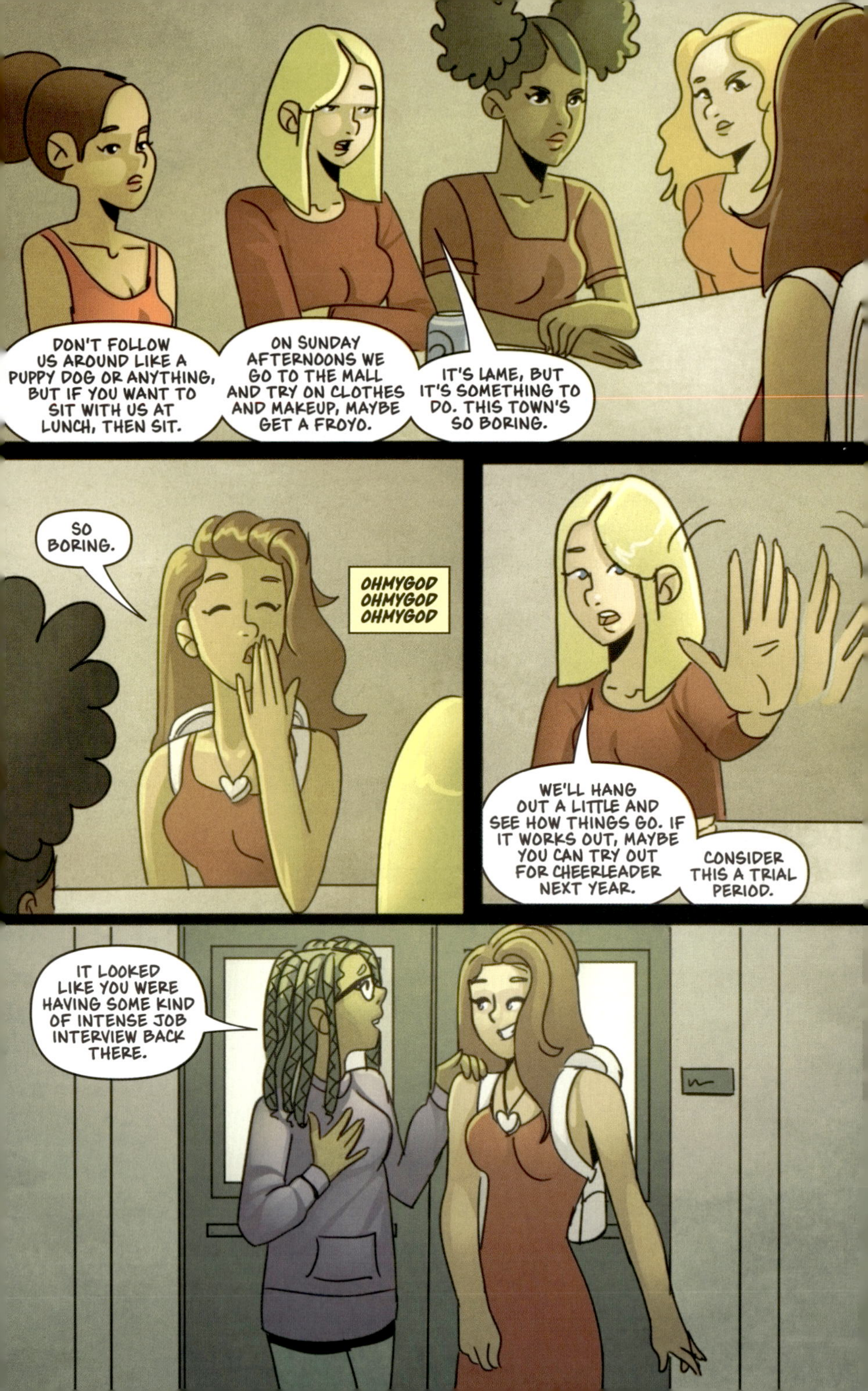
DON'T FOLLOW US AROUND LIKE A PUPPY DOG OR ANYTHING, BUT IF YOU WANT TO SIT WITH US AT LUNCH, THEN SIT.
ON SUNDAY AFTERNOONS WE GO TO THE MALL AND TRY ON CLOTHES AND MAKEUP, MAYBE GET A FROYO.
IT'S LAME, BUT IT'S SOMETHING TO DO. THIS TOWN'S SO BORING.
SO BORING.
OHMYGOD OHMYGOD OHMYGOD
WE'LL HANG OUT A LITTLE AND SEE HOW THINGS GO. IF IT WORKS OUT, MAYBE YOU CAN TRY OUT FOR CHEERLEADER NEXT YEAR.
CONSIDER THIS A TRIAL PERIOD.
IT LOOKED LIKE YOU WERE HAVING SOME KIND OF INTENSE JOB INTERVIEW BACK THERE.

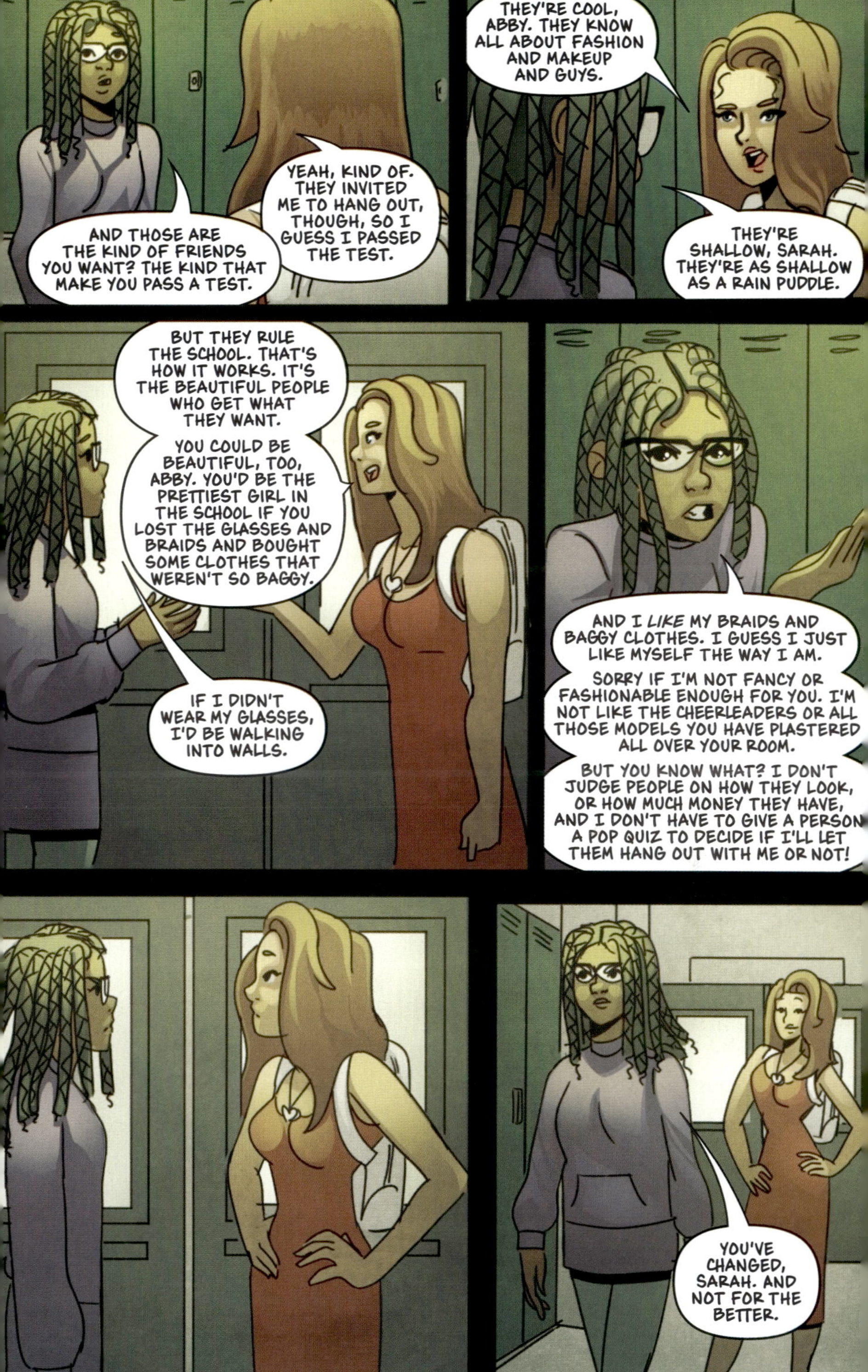
YEAH, KIND OF. THEY INVITED ME TO HANG OUT, THOUGH, SO I GUESS I PASSED THE TEST.
AND THOSE ARE THE KIND OF FRIENDS YOU WANT? THE KIND THAT MAKE YOU PASS A TEST.
THEY'RE COOL, ABBY. THEY KNOW ALL ABOUT FASHION AND MAKEUP AND GUYS.
THEY'RE SHALLOW, SARAH. THEY'RE AS SHALLOW AS A RAIN PUDDLE.
BUT THEY RULE THE SCHOOL. THAT'S HOW IT WORKS. IT'S THE BEAUTIFUL PEOPLE WHO GET WHAT THEY WANT.
YOU COULD BE BEAUTIFUL, TOO, ABBY. YOU'D BE THE PRETTIEST GIRL IN THE SCHOOL IF YOU LOST THE GLASSES AND BRAIDS AND BOUGHT SOME CLOTHES THAT WEREN'T SO BAGGY.
IF I DIDN'T WEAR MY GLASSES, I'D BE WALKING INTO WALLS.
AND I *LIKE* MY BRAIDS AND BAGGY CLOTHES. I GUESS I JUST LIKE MYSELF THE WAY I AM.
SORRY IF I'M NOT FANCY OR FASHIONABLE ENOUGH FOR YOU. I'M NOT LIKE THE CHEERLEADERS OR ALL THOSE MODELS YOU HAVE PLASTERED ALL OVER YOUR ROOM.
BUT YOU KNOW WHAT? I DON'T JUDGE PEOPLE ON HOW THEY LOOK, OR HOW MUCH MONEY THEY HAVE, AND I DON'T HAVE TO GIVE A PERSON A POP QUIZ TO DECIDE IF I'LL LET THEM HANG OUT WITH ME OR NOT!
YOU'VE CHANGED, SARAH. AND NOT FOR THE BETTER.

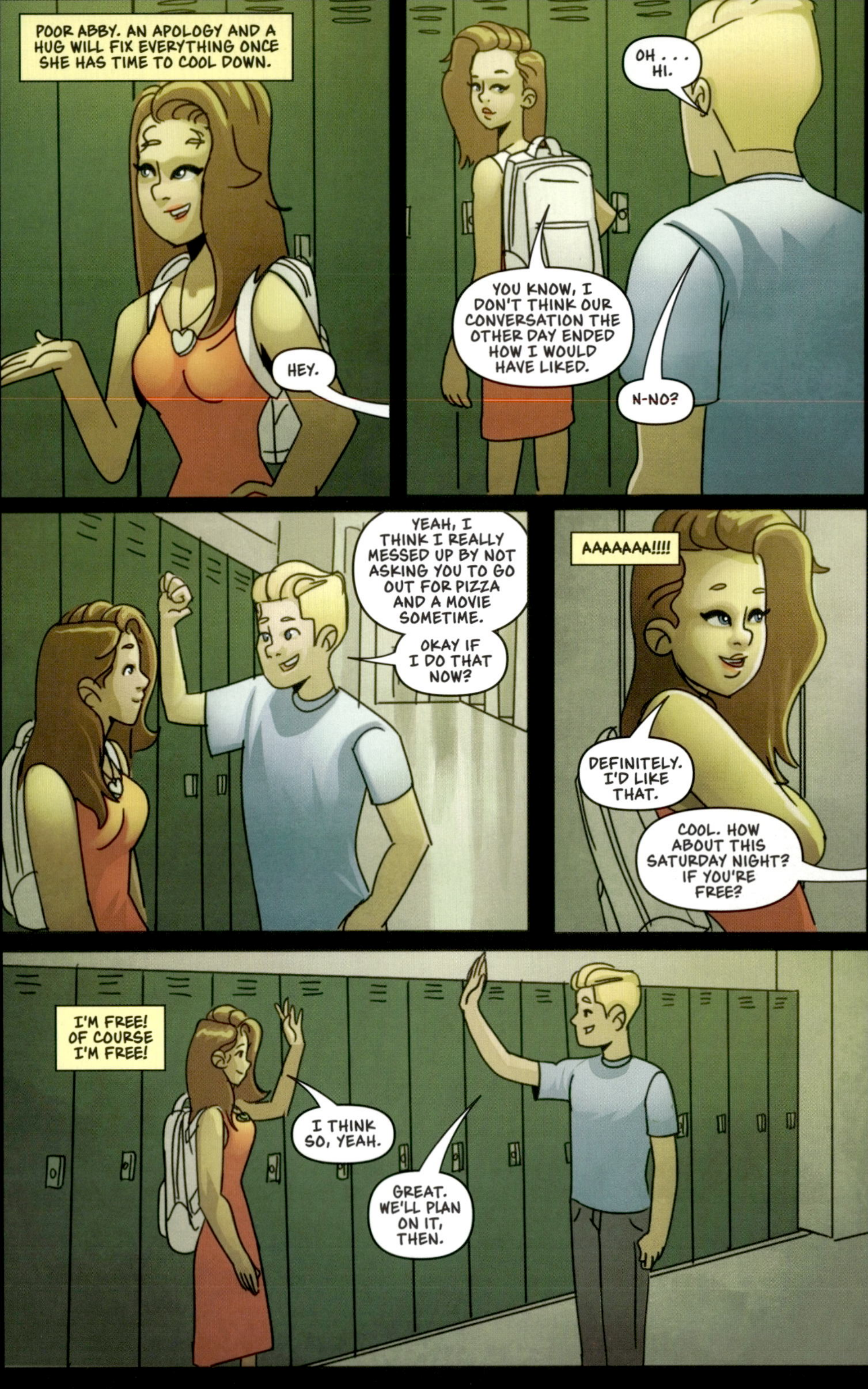

POOR ABBY. AN APOLOGY AND A HUG WILL FIX EVERYTHING ONCE SHE HAS TIME TO COOL DOWN.

HEY.

OH . . . HI.

YOU KNOW, I DON'T THINK OUR CONVERSATION THE OTHER DAY ENDED HOW I WOULD HAVE LIKED.

N-NO?

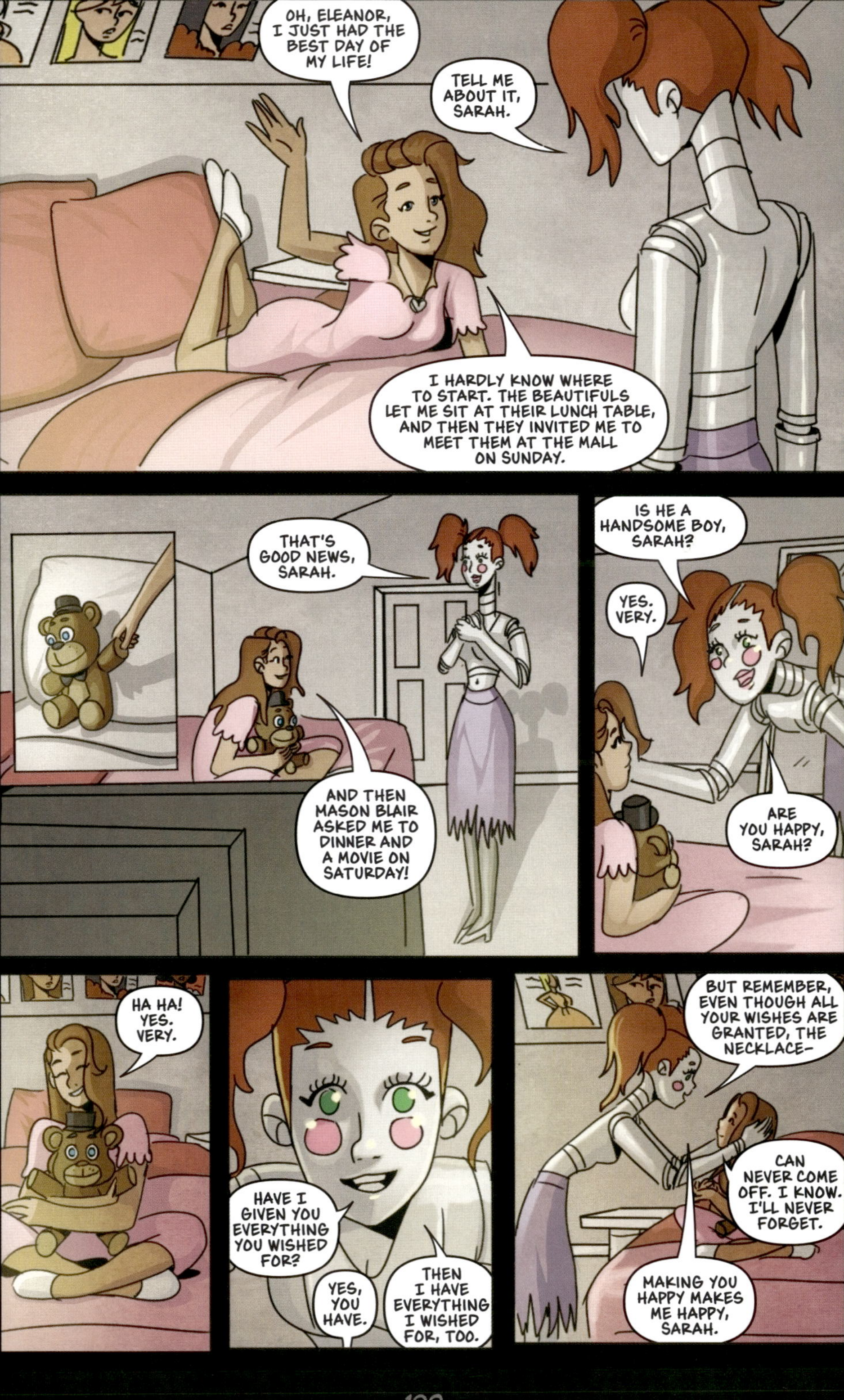

OH, ELEANOR, I JUST HAD THE BEST DAY OF MY LIFE!
TELL ME ABOUT IT, SARAH.
I HARDLY KNOW WHERE TO START. THE BEAUTIFULS LET ME SIT AT THEIR LUNCH TABLE, AND THEN THEY INVITED ME TO MEET THEM AT THE MALL ON SUNDAY.
THAT'S GOOD NEWS, SARAH.
AND THEN MASON BLAIR ASKED ME TO DINNER AND A MOVIE ON SATURDAY!
IS HE A HANDSOME BOY, SARAH?
YES. VERY.
ARE YOU HAPPY, SARAH?
HA HA! YES. VERY.
HAVE I GIVEN YOU EVERYTHING YOU WISHED FOR?
YES, YOU HAVE.
THEN I HAVE EVERYTHING I WISHED FOR, TOO.
BUT REMEMBER, EVEN THOUGH ALL YOUR WISHES ARE GRANTED, THE NECKLACE–
CAN NEVER COME OFF. I KNOW. I'LL NEVER FORGET.
MAKING YOU HAPPY MAKES ME HAPPY, SARAH.

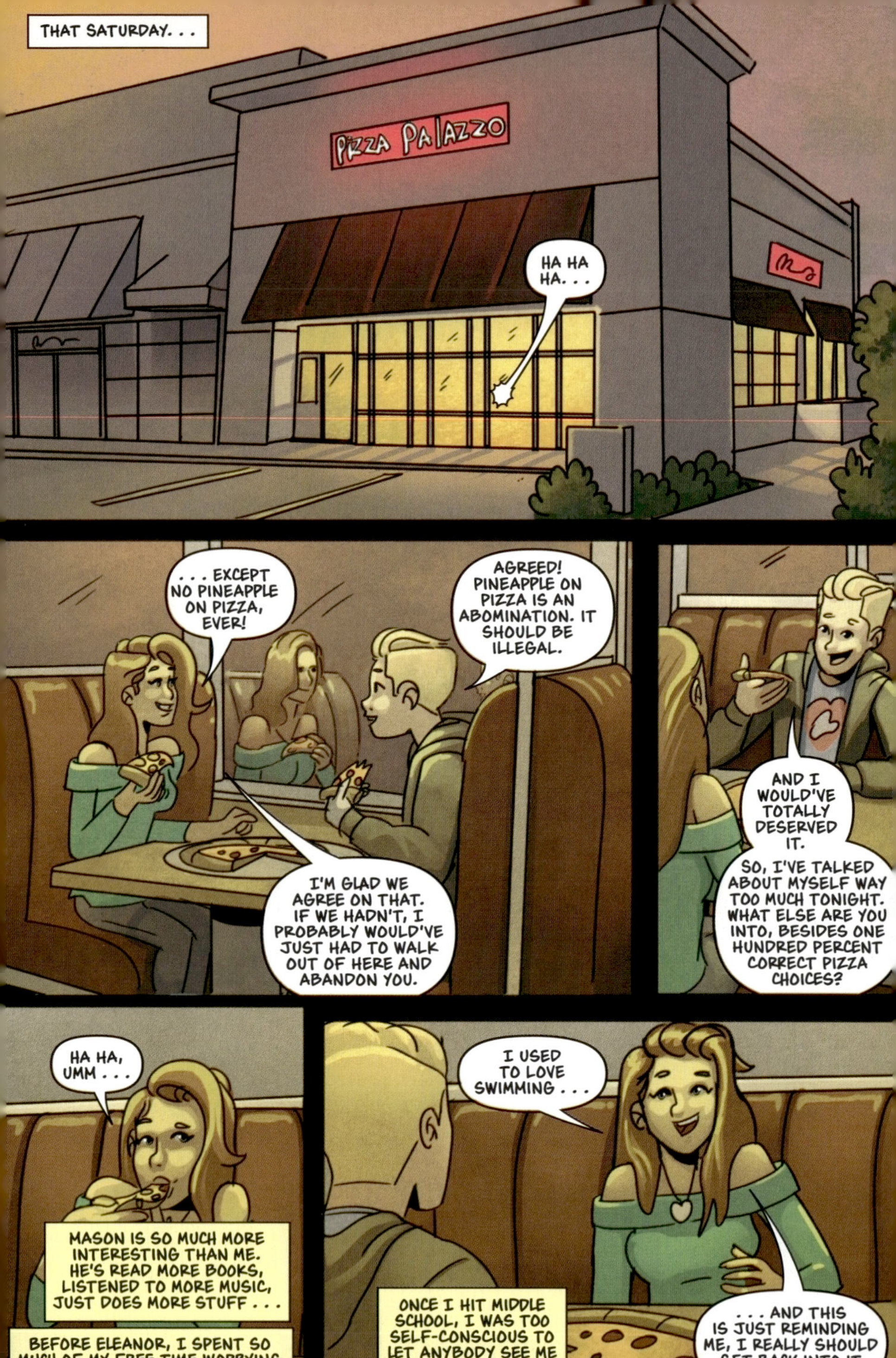
THAT SATURDAY. . .
PIZZA PALAZZO
HA HA HA. . .
. . . EXCEPT NO PINEAPPLE ON PIZZA, EVER!
AGREED! PINEAPPLE ON PIZZA IS AN ABOMINATION. IT SHOULD BE ILLEGAL.
I'M GLAD WE AGREE ON THAT. IF WE HADN'T, I PROBABLY WOULD'VE JUST HAD TO WALK OUT OF HERE AND ABANDON YOU.
AND I WOULD'VE TOTALLY DESERVED IT.
SO, I'VE TALKED ABOUT MYSELF WAY TOO MUCH TONIGHT. WHAT ELSE ARE YOU INTO, BESIDES ONE HUNDRED PERCENT CORRECT PIZZA CHOICES?
HA HA, UMM . . .
MASON IS SO MUCH MORE INTERESTING THAN ME. HE'S READ MORE BOOKS, LISTENED TO MORE MUSIC, JUST DOES MORE STUFF . . .
BEFORE ELEANOR, I SPENT SO MUCH OF MY FREE TIME WORRYING ABOUT MY APPEARANCE, I DIDN'T DO ANYTHING ELSE!
I USED TO LOVE SWIMMING . . .
ONCE I HIT MIDDLE SCHOOL, I WAS TOO SELF-CONSCIOUS TO LET ANYBODY SEE ME IN A BATHING SUIT.
. . . AND THIS IS JUST REMINDING ME, I REALLY SHOULD GET BACK INTO IT AGAIN!

AT LEAST I'M NOT TOTALLY BORING.
HE SEEMS INTERESTED IN LITERALLY ANYTHING I HAVE TO SAY.
AND HE'S NOT JUST CUTE! HE'S NICE, AND FUNNY, AND–
. . . AND HOW DO I KEEP HAVING THE BEST DAYS OF MY LIFE, ONE AFTER ANOTHER?

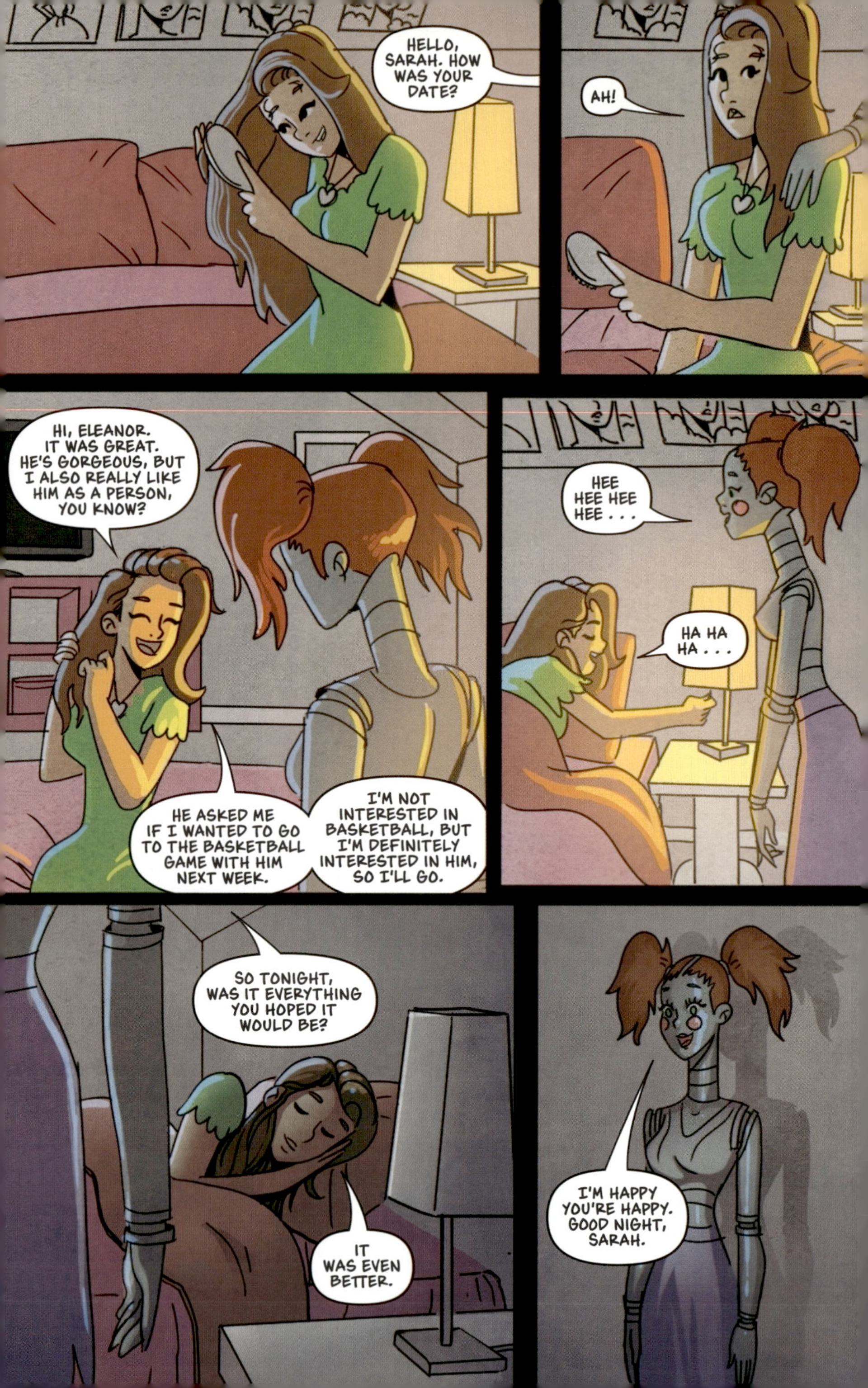
HELLO, SARAH. HOW WAS YOUR DATE?
AH!
HI, ELEANOR. IT WAS GREAT. HE'S GORGEOUS, BUT I ALSO REALLY LIKE HIM AS A PERSON, YOU KNOW?
HE ASKED ME IF I WANTED TO GO TO THE BASKETBALL GAME WITH HIM NEXT WEEK.
I'M NOT INTERESTED IN BASKETBALL, BUT I'M DEFINITELY INTERESTED IN HIM, SO I'LL GO.
HEE HEE HEE HEE . . .
HA HA HA . . .
SO TONIGHT, WAS IT EVERYTHING YOU HOPED IT WOULD BE?
IT WAS EVEN BETTER.
I'M HAPPY YOU'RE HAPPY. GOOD NIGHT, SARAH.

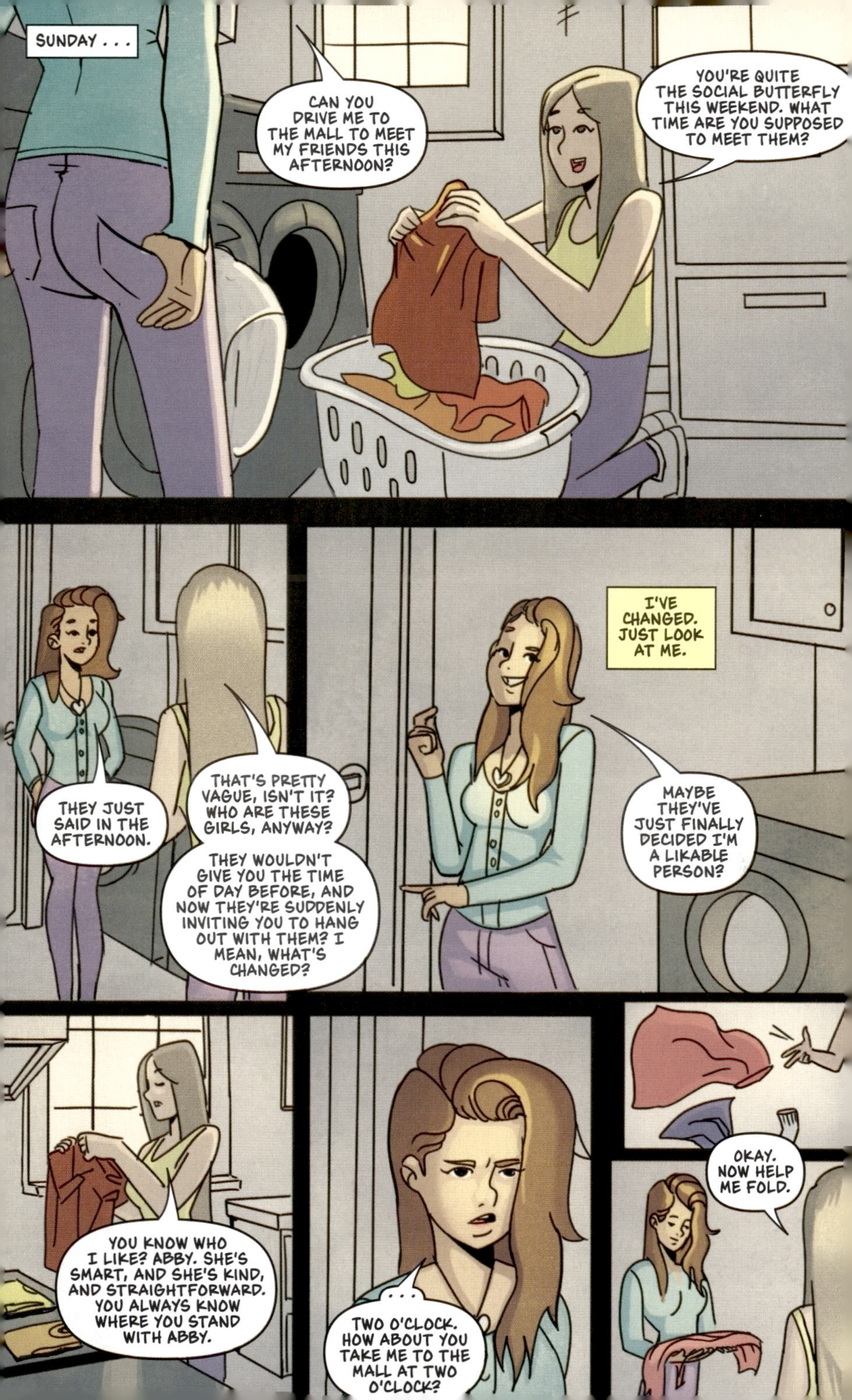
SUNDAY . . .
CAN YOU DRIVE ME TO THE MALL TO MEET MY FRIENDS THIS AFTERNOON?
YOU'RE QUITE THE SOCIAL BUTTERFLY THIS WEEKEND. WHAT TIME ARE YOU SUPPOSED TO MEET THEM?
THEY JUST SAID IN THE AFTERNOON.
THAT'S PRETTY VAGUE, ISN'T IT? WHO ARE THESE GIRLS, ANYWAY?
THEY WOULDN'T GIVE YOU THE TIME OF DAY BEFORE, AND NOW THEY'RE SUDDENLY INVITING YOU TO HANG OUT WITH THEM? I MEAN, WHAT'S CHANGED?
I'VE CHANGED. JUST LOOK AT ME.
MAYBE THEY'VE JUST FINALLY DECIDED I'M A LIKABLE PERSON?
YOU KNOW WHO I LIKE? ABBY. SHE'S SMART, AND SHE'S KIND, AND STRAIGHTFORWARD. YOU ALWAYS KNOW WHERE YOU STAND WITH ABBY.
. . .
TWO O'CLOCK. HOW ABOUT YOU TAKE ME TO THE MALL AT TWO O'CLOCK?
OKAY. NOW HELP ME FOLD.

TOWN CENTER
SO . . . NOT ONLY DID THEY NOT TELL ME WHEN TO MEET THEM, THEY DIDN'T SAY WHERE, EITHER.
I COULD TEXT LYDIA, BUT THAT COULD BLOW THE "TEST."
MAYBE I SHOULD JUST TRY THE MOST EXPENSIVE STORE IN THE MALL.
BINGO. I KNEW THEY WOULDN'T HANG OUT SOMEPLACE CHEAP.
SARAH, YOU MADE IT!
HI.
OOH, SARAH, YOU SHOULD TRY ON THIS LIPSTICK. IT'S PINK WITH SPARKLES. IT WOULD LOOK PERFECT WITH YOUR SKIN TONE.
IT LOOKS LIKE LIPSTICK A PRINCESS WOULD WEAR.
IT REALLY DOES. HER ROYAL HIGHNESS, PRINCESS SARAH.
FORTY DOLLARS!!! THAT'S MORE THAN MY ENTIRE OUTFIT COST!
I'LL THINK ABOUT IT.
OH, GO ON. TREAT YOURSELF.
I WANT TO BROWSE AROUND A LITTLE MORE FIRST, SINCE I JUST GOT HERE.

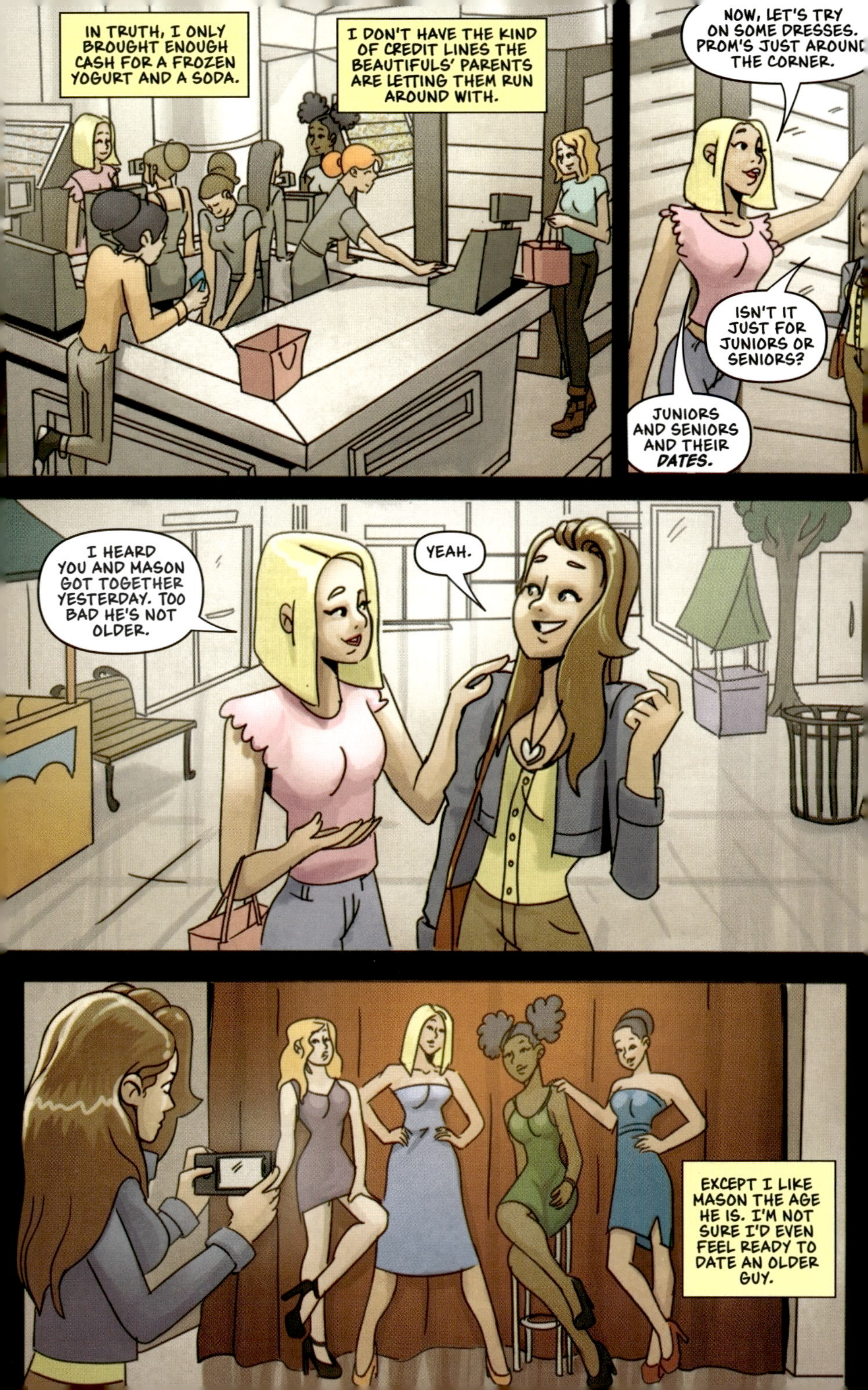

IN TRUTH, I ONLY BROUGHT ENOUGH CASH FOR A FROZEN YOGURT AND A SODA.

I DON'T HAVE THE KIND OF CREDIT LINES THE BEAUTIFULS' PARENTS ARE LETTING THEM RUN AROUND WITH.

NOW, LET'S TRY ON SOME DRESSES. PROM'S JUST AROUND THE CORNER.

ISN'T IT JUST FOR JUNIORS OR SENIORS?

JUNIORS AND SENIORS AND THEIR *DATES.*

I HEARD YOU AND MASON GOT TOGETHER YESTERDAY. TOO BAD HE'S NOT OLDER.

YEAH.

WERE YOU GIRLS ACTUALLY INTERESTED IN BUYING ANY OF THESE DRESSES, OR ARE YOU JUST PLAYING DRESS-UP?
HA HA HA HA HA
SORRYYYYYY!
I DON'T THINK THAT SALESLADY LIKED US VERY MUCH.
WHO CARES? SHE DOESN'T GET TO JUDGE ME. SHE JUST WORKS IN A STORE. SHE MAKES MINIMUM WAGE IF SHE'S LUCKY. I BET SHE CAN'T EVEN AFFORD TO BUY THE CLOTHES SHE SELLS.
WASN'T SHE JUST TRYING TO DO HER JOB?
DO YOU GIRLS INTEND TO BUY ANYTHING, OR ARE YOU JUST PLAYING DRESS-UP?
HA HA HA HA
JILLIAN AND EMMA LEFT THEIR DRESSES IN A CRUMPLED PILE. THE SALESLADY WILL PROBABLY JUST HAVE TO CLEAN UP AFTER THEM.
BUT WHO AM I TO CRITICIZE THEM? IT'S EXCITING, LIKE BEING A GUEST ON A REALITY TV SHOW.

IT'S AN HONOR JUST TO BE INVITED.
MALL
TOWN CENTER
AND NOW ANOTHER DATE WITH MASON? I'M THE LUCKIEST GIRL ALIVE . . .
IT'S STRANGE . . . WE WERE SUPPOSED TO GO TO A BASKETBALL GAME.
I DON'T CARE. I'D BE HAPPY ANYWHERE WITH HIM, ESPECIALLY WHEN HE HOLDS MY . . .
. . . HAND.

AAAAAAAH!!!
GASP
JUST A DREAM.
JUST A . . .

AH!
ELEANOR! DID I MAKE A NOISE IN MY SLEEP?
NO, SARAH.
THEN WHAT ARE YOU DOING STANDING OVER MY BED?
I DO THIS EVERY NIGHT. I WATCH OVER YOU. I KEEP YOU SAFE.
UH, OKAY. THANKS, I GUESS.
YOU'RE WELCOME, SARAH. GOOD NIGHT.

MONDAY . . .
CAN YOU BELIEVE WHAT SHE'S WEARING? SHE DRESSES LIKE A PRESCHOOLER.
LIKE A PRESCHOOLER FROM A POOR FAMILY.
OH NO, THEY'RE TALKING ABOUT ABBY . . .
THAT'S ABBY. SHE'S REALLY NICE.
SHE'S BEEN MY FRIEND SINCE KINDERGARTEN-
YEAH, BUT YOU'VE BOUGHT NEW CLOTHES SINCE KINDERGARTEN AND SHE HASN'T-
SARAH?!

HA HA HA HA HA!
SARAH, THAT WAS HILARIOUS! WHAT A KLUTZ!
CRASH KLANG BANG
CLANG CLANG CLANG
WHAT'S THAT SOUND? IT'S LIKE IT'S COMING FROM INSIDE ME . . .
SHE HIT THE FLOOR LIKE A TON OF BRICKS.
HOW EMBARRASSING . . .
I CAN'T MOVE. I'M SHAKING. WHAT'S WRONG?
WHY WON'T THEY HELP ME?

HA
HA HA . . .
HA . . .
. . . UHH . . .
AAAAAH!!!!
WHAT'S HAPPENING TO HER? I DON'T UNDERSTAND!
THE NECKLACE . . .
I DON'T KNOW! SOMEBODY NEEDS TO DO SOMETHING!
GET A TEACHER, QUICK!

WHAT . . .
WHAAATSTS WRONG WITH MEE . . .
01 2220

I'VE-
I'VE GOT
TO GO.
HERE,
LET ME HELP
YOU . . .
YOU
DROPPED
THIS.
THANK
YOU, ABBY.
YOU'RE A GOOD
FRIEND.
I HAVE TO
GET HOME.
ELEANOR
WILL KNOW
WHAT TO DO.

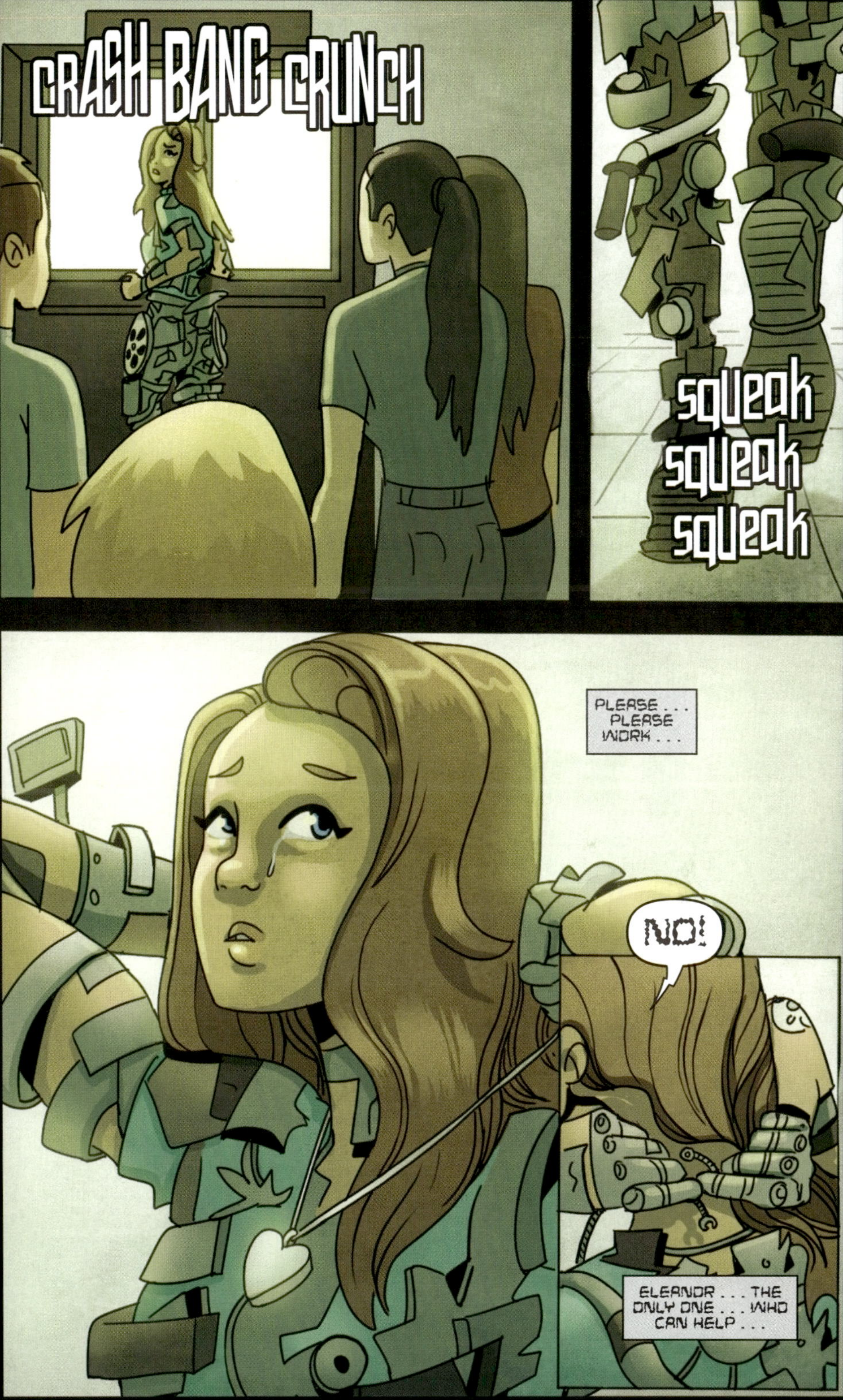

PLEASE . . . PLEASE WORK . . .

NO!

ELEANOR . . . THE ONLY ONE . . . WHO CAN HELP . . .

ELEANOR! ELEANOR!
ELEANOR?!
WHERE IS SHE?
EH-NAH?
IN HERE?

THUD

WHAAA . . .

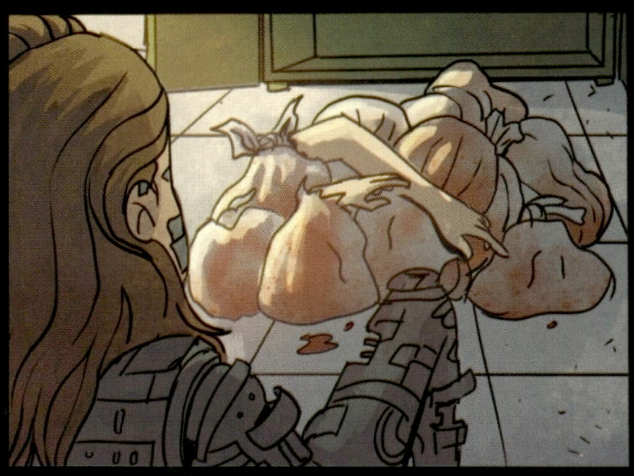

N . . .
NNNN . . .

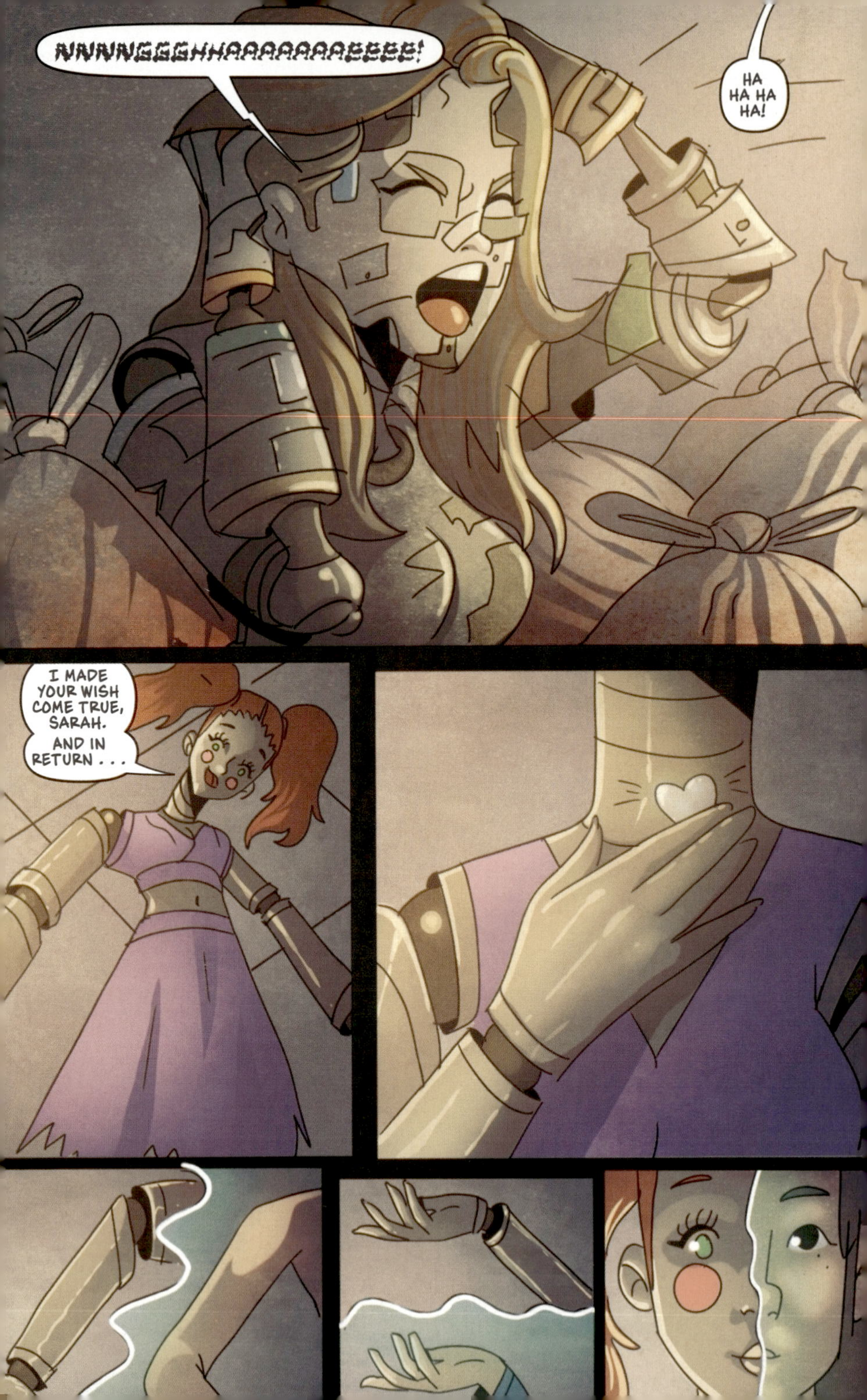
NNNNGGGHHAAAAAAAAEEEE!
HA HA HA HA!
I MADE YOUR WISH COME TRUE, SARAH. AND IN RETURN . . .

WELL, YOU CERTAINLY MADE MY WISHES COME TRUE.
WHAT DO YOU THINK? NOT SO BAD-LOOKING AFTER ALL, HUH?
ABBY . . . WAS . . . RIGHT . . .
HA HA HA . . .
YES, ABBY WAS RIGHT ABOUT A LOT OF THINGS.
BYE, BYE!
GO TO SLEEP, GO TO SLEEP . . .
GO TO SLEEP, MY SWEET SARAH . . .

OUT OF STOCK

SHE'S BEEN PLOTTING THIS WHOLE TIME. I SHOULD HAVE KNOWN. SHE WAITED UNTIL I LET MY GUARD DOWN.
I CAN FEEL MY SOUL SLIPPING AWAY. IT'S OOZING OUT OF MY PORES, OSCAR.
C'MON, MR. DEVEREAUX, YOU DON'T REALLY BELIEVE THAT.
BUT WHY WOULD SHE DO THAT? SHE LOVES YOU. SHE'S SHARED YOUR ROOM EVERY NIGHT FOR YEARS. DON'T YOU THINK IF SHE WANTED YOUR SOUL, SHE WOULD HAVE TAKEN IT BY NOW?
TRUST CANNOT BE RUSHED, YOUNG MAN. GOOD FORTUNE CANNOT BE PREDICTED.
MAYBE MARILYN ISN'T STEALING YOUR SOUL. MAYBE SHE'S GUARDING IT. YOU KNOW, LIKE HOLDING IT FOR SAFEKEEPING.
A TEMPTING THEORY, BUT SHE SHOULD HAVE ASKED PERMISSION.
WELL, MARILYN? WHAT DO YOU HAVE TO SAY FOR YOURSELF?

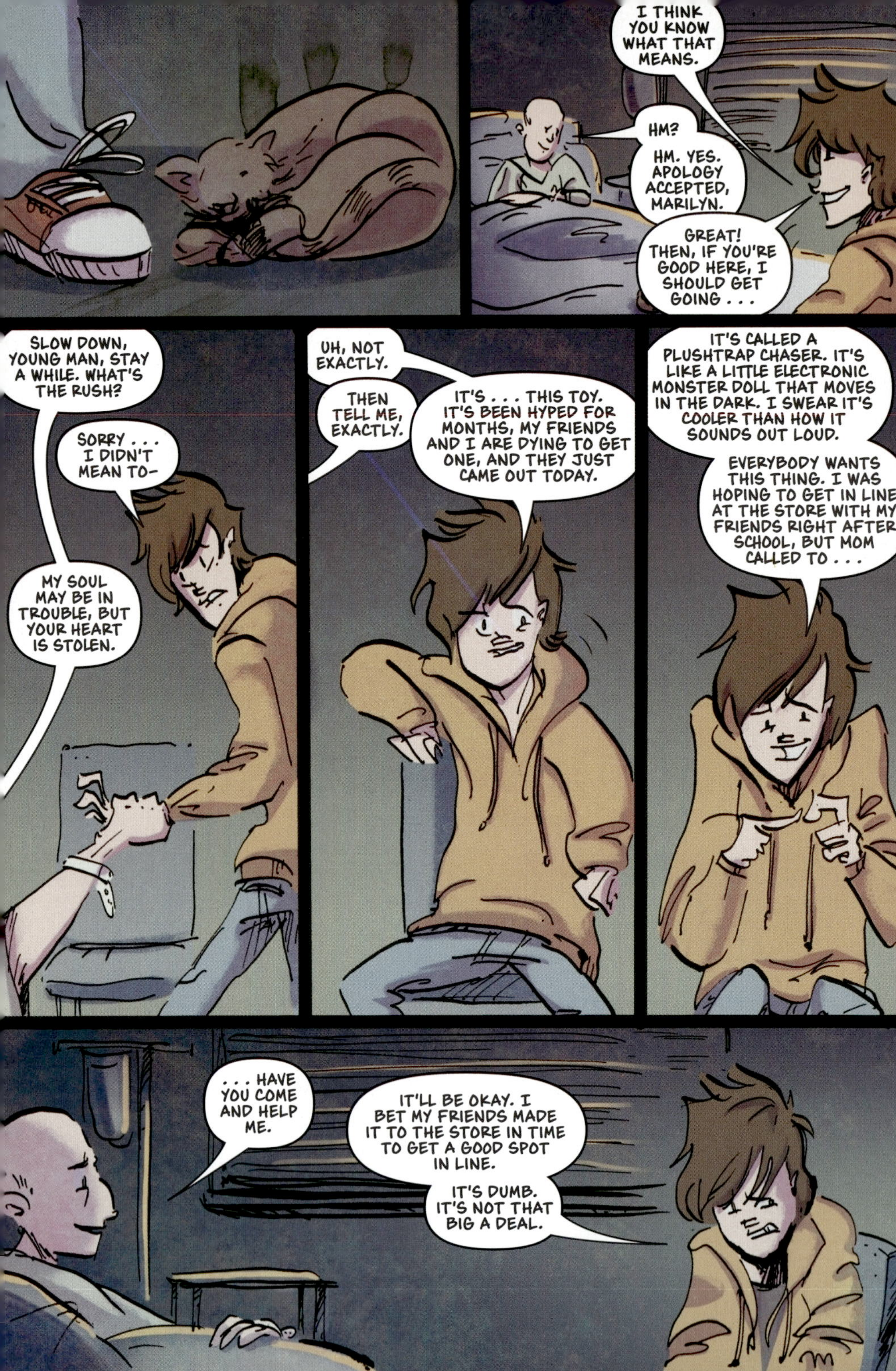
I THINK YOU KNOW WHAT THAT MEANS.
HM?
HM. YES. APOLOGY ACCEPTED, MARILYN.
GREAT! THEN, IF YOU'RE GOOD HERE, I SHOULD GET GOING . . .
SLOW DOWN, YOUNG MAN, STAY A WHILE. WHAT'S THE RUSH?
SORRY . . . I DIDN'T MEAN TO-
MY SOUL MAY BE IN TROUBLE, BUT YOUR HEART IS STOLEN.
UH, NOT EXACTLY.
THEN TELL ME, EXACTLY.
IT'S . . . THIS TOY. IT'S BEEN HYPED FOR MONTHS, MY FRIENDS AND I ARE DYING TO GET ONE, AND THEY JUST CAME OUT TODAY.
IT'S CALLED A PLUSHTRAP CHASER. IT'S LIKE A LITTLE ELECTRONIC MONSTER DOLL THAT MOVES IN THE DARK. I SWEAR IT'S COOLER THAN HOW IT SOUNDS OUT LOUD.
EVERYBODY WANTS THIS THING. I WAS HOPING TO GET IN LINE AT THE STORE WITH MY FRIENDS RIGHT AFTER SCHOOL, BUT MOM CALLED TO . . .
. . . HAVE YOU COME AND HELP ME.
IT'LL BE OKAY. I BET MY FRIENDS MADE IT TO THE STORE IN TIME TO GET A GOOD SPOT IN LINE.
IT'S DUMB. IT'S NOT THAT BIG A DEAL.

THE TOY IS ONLY THE STEM THAT BREAKS THE GROUND.
THE REASON FOR THE WANTING IS WHAT LIES UNDERNEATH. IT'S THE SOIL THAT FEEDS THE WANT.
I THINK YOU HAVE TILLED QUITE A LOT OF SOIL. SO MUCH WANTING.
BUT YOU'VE NEVER BEEN ABLE TO PLUCK THE FRUITS OF YOUR LABOR FROM YOUR GROUND, HAVE YOU?
IT'S JUST THAT IT'S BEEN TOUGH FOR MOM SINCE DAD . . . UH . . .
MOM HAS TO RELY ON ME. AND THAT MEANS GIVING THINGS UP SOMETIMES.
THE BEST CULTIVATORS ARE THE ONES WHO KNOW WHEN IT'S TIME TO PICK THE CROPS.
MR. D . . . I'M REALLY NOT SURE WHAT-
I'M TRYING TO TELL YOU TO QUIT TILLING.
. . . IT'S TIME . . .

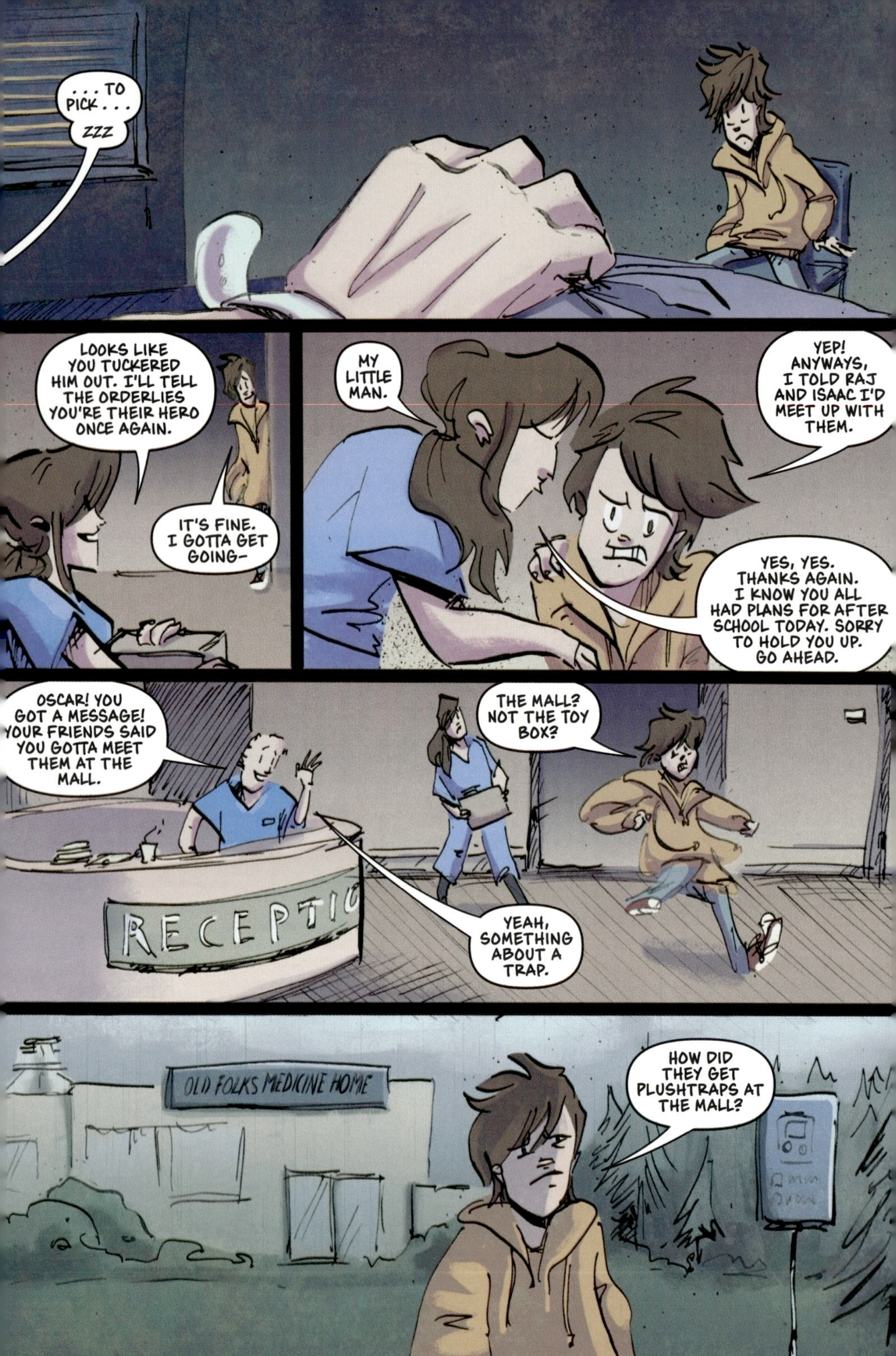
. . . TO PICK . . . ZZZ
LOOKS LIKE YOU TUCKERED HIM OUT. I'LL TELL THE ORDERLIES YOU'RE THEIR HERO ONCE AGAIN.
IT'S FINE. I GOTTA GET GOING-
MY LITTLE MAN.
YEP! ANYWAYS, I TOLD RAJ AND ISAAC I'D MEET UP WITH THEM.
YES, YES. THANKS AGAIN. I KNOW YOU ALL HAD PLANS FOR AFTER SCHOOL TODAY. SORRY TO HOLD YOU UP. GO AHEAD.
OSCAR! YOU GOT A MESSAGE! YOUR FRIENDS SAID YOU GOTTA MEET THEM AT THE MALL.
THE MALL? NOT THE TOY BOX?
YEAH, SOMETHING ABOUT A TRAP.
RECEPTIO
OLD FOLKS MEDICINE HOME
HOW DID THEY GET PLUSHTRAPS AT THE MALL?

THE EMPORIUM'S ALMOST GONE BANKRUPT THREE TIMES.
I HOPE THEY'RE RIGHT ABOUT-
OKAY, SO THEY WERE RIGHT. THIS IS THE SPOT.
THE EMPORIUM
OSCAR! OVER HERE!
HEY! THERE'S A SYSTEM HERE, KID!
SORRY! THEY SAVED MY SPOT!

DUDE, WE TRIED THE TOY BOX, MARBLES, AND THAT PLACE ON TWENTY-THIRD AND SAN JUAN.
WE EVEN WENT TO THAT WEIRD ORGANIC PLACE ON FIFTH STREET THAT ONLY SELLS WOODEN TOYS.
IF THEY EVER HAD IT AT ALL, THEY SOLD OUT IN, LIKE, FIVE MINUTES.
T-CHUNKT TK TK TK TK TK
BUT THE EMPORIUM HAS THEM?
OOF!
SURE LOOKS LIKE IT.
I HOPE THEY HAVE ENOUGH . . .

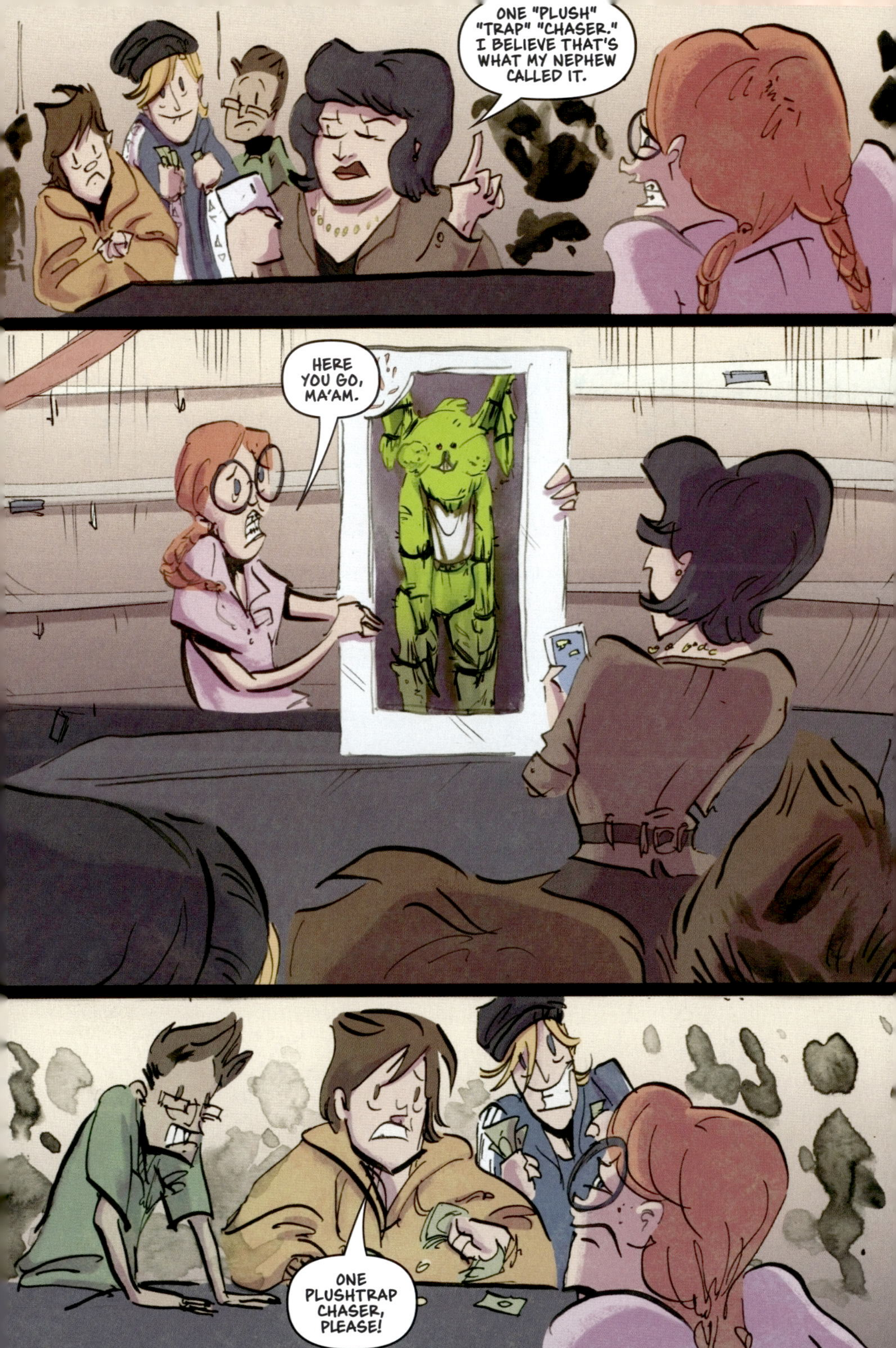
ONE "PLUSH" "TRAP" "CHASER." I BELIEVE THAT'S WHAT MY NEPHEW CALLED IT.
HERE YOU GO, MA'AM.
ONE PLUSHTRAP CHASER, PLEASE!

IF THERE'S ONLY ONE LEFT, WE CAN SPLIT IT.
SORRY . . .
WHAT DO YOU MEAN, "SORRY"?
NO . . . NONONONONONO . . .
WE'RE . . .
. . . SOLD OUT.
WHAT?! NO! ARE YOU KIDDING ME?! BOOOOO! NOO!!!
IT CAN'T BE!

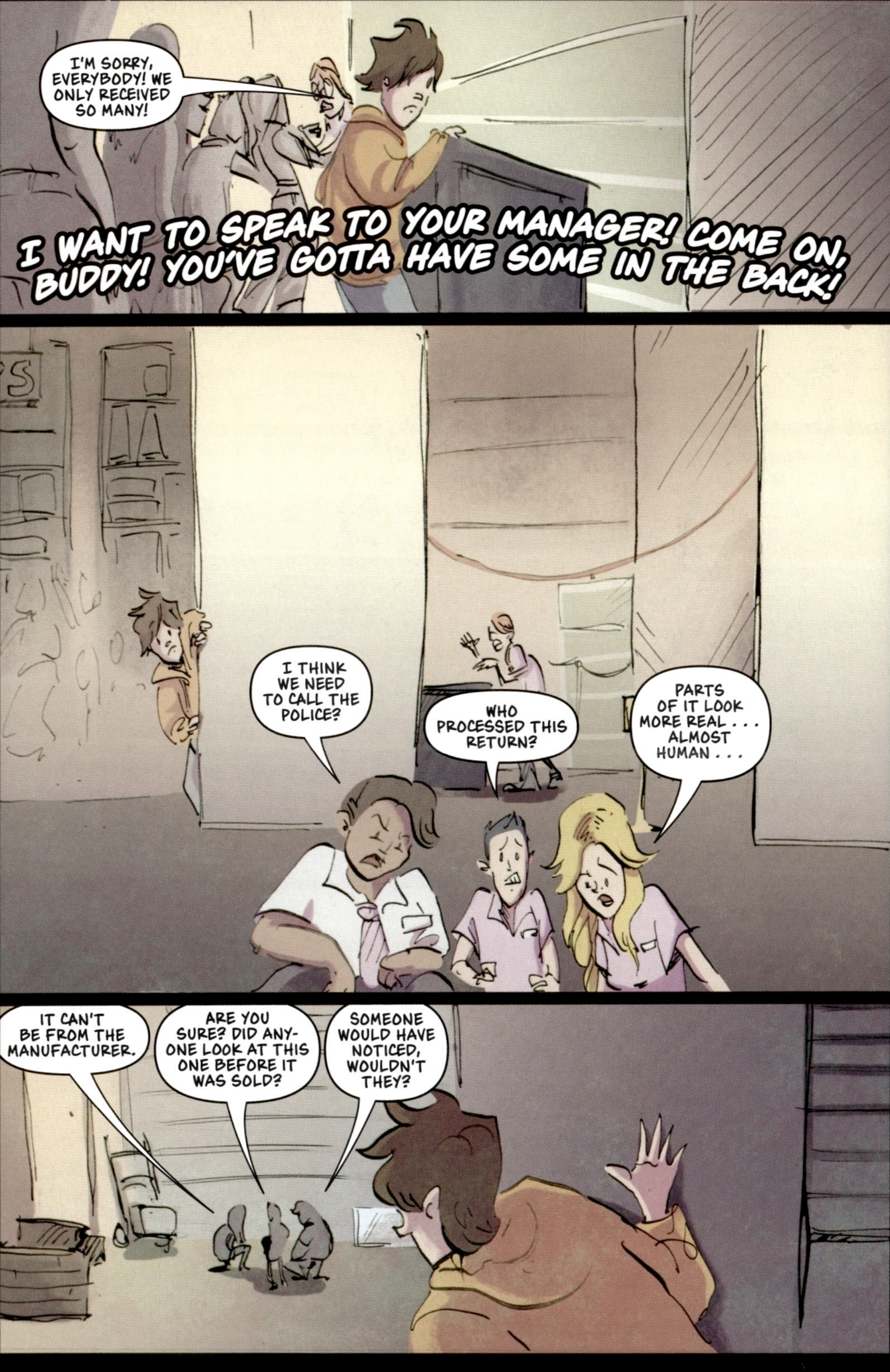
I'M SORRY, EVERYBODY! WE ONLY RECEIVED SO MANY!
I WANT TO SPEAK TO YOUR MANAGER! COME ON, BUDDY! YOU'VE GOTTA HAVE SOME IN THE BACK!
I THINK WE NEED TO CALL THE POLICE?
WHO PROCESSED THIS RETURN?
PARTS OF IT LOOK MORE REAL . . . ALMOST HUMAN . . .
IT CAN'T BE FROM THE MANUFACTURER.
ARE YOU SURE? DID ANY-ONE LOOK AT THIS ONE BEFORE IT WAS SOLD?
SOMEONE WOULD HAVE NOTICED, WOULDN'T THEY?

I STILL THINK WE SHOULD CALL THE POLICE.
AND SAY WHAT? "SOMEONE RETURNED A TOY, AND FUNNY STORY, NOW THE TOY LOOKS TOO LIFELIKE! HELP, OFFICER, HELP!"
IT'S NOT JUST LIFELIKE. IT'S . . . DISTURBING–
HELP! THEY'RE ABOUT TO REVOLT!
I'M SORRY, EVERYONE. WE ARE SOLD OUT OF THE PLUSHTRAP CHASER . . .
YOUR CLERK SAID YOU HAD ENOUGH FOR EVERYONE!
I DOUBT HE SAID THAT. PEOPLE, PLEASE CALM DOWN!

YOU'VE GOT A LOT OF SHIPPING CONTAINERS BACK THERE! DID YOU MISS ANY? WHAT ARE YOU HIDING?!
IF YOU DON'T ALL BREAK IT UP AND LEAVE, I'M CALLING SECURITY!
QUIT TILLING . . .
IT'S TIME TO PICK.

JUST LET US IN THERE TO CHECK!
SIR, GO HOME. THERE'S NOTHING HERE. GO CHECK EBAY OR SOMETHING.
I'M BUYING THIS ONE! THANKS!
DUDE, WHAT ARE YOU DOING?!
STOP! *STOP!*
HEY! THAT ONE'S NOT FOR SALE!

SECURITY!
OH MAN, THE GUARDS! WHAT IS GOING ON, OSCAR?!
STOP THEM!
I'LL TELL YOU WHEN WE GET HOME! HURRY!
ALMOST THERE . . .

STOP . . .
COUGH
THAT'S . . . THAT'S . . .
PRIVATE PROPERTY . . .

WE MADE IT!

OOOOF!

HUFF HUFF HUFF

TECHNICALLY . . .
HUFF
. . . IT WASN'T STEALING. I LEFT THE MONEY.

YOU'RE AN IDIOT.
YEAH, I KNOW.
SO ARE WE GOING TO OPEN IT?

OKAY, LET'S SEE WHAT THIS BEAST CAN DO.
UH . . .
HM.
I DON'T KNOW WHY, BUT IT'S NOT EXACTLY HOW I'D IMAGINED IT.
IS IT JUST ME, OR DO THE TEETH LOOK WRONG? LIKE THEY'RE . . . REAL. HUMAN.
AND WHAT'S WITH THE EYES . . .
EW!
IT'S SQUISHY!
THAT'S WHY THEY WERE SO FREAKED OUT . . .
I'VE GOTTA TELL YOU SOMETHING I OVERHEARD IN THE STORE.
THE EMPLOYEES WERE TALKING ABOUT WHAT TO DO WITH THIS. IT WAS RETURNED, BUT NONE OF THEM KNEW FROM WHOM, AND THEY WERE GOING TO CALL THE COPS BECAUSE . . .

BECAUSE THE EYES AND TEETH ARE *HUMAN?!*
I GUESS WHEN YOU SAY IT OUT LOUD, IT SOUNDS A LITTLE RIDICULOUS.
TOTALLY.
I MEAN, IT'S NOT LIKE ANY ONE OF US GOT A REALLY GOOD LOOK AT ONE OF THESE CLOSE-UP. THEY'RE PROBABLY ALL-
NIGHTMARISH?
MAYBE IF WE SEE IT IN ACTION, WE'LL FEEL BETTER.
WHY NOT?
NOTHING.
THERE'S A BATTERY COMPARTMENT BACK HERE . . .
BATTERY ACID. YUCK.
I GUESS THE OLD OWNER LEFT THE BATTERY IN. AND IS THAT A SPEAKER? DOES IT TALK?
NAH. NOT IN ANY OF THE ADS.
WHAT DOES A RABBIT EVEN SOUND LIKE?

LET'S TRY A FRESH BATTERY.
MAYBE IT JUST NEEDS SOME HELP MOVING? LET'S OPEN ITS MOUTH, GET THE SNAPPING ACTION GOING.
GOOD IDEA-
SNAP
TELL ME IT DIDN'T TAKE A BITE OUT OF A KNIFE.
IT DIDN'T BREAK THE KNIFE, RAJ. I BROKE IT.

WALK DARK! IN LIGHT
HANG ON, HANG ON . . .
GUYS, IT ONLY WORKS WHEN THE LIGHTS ARE OFF.
OHHHHH . . .
IT'S JUST NOT DARK ENOUGH YET.
IT PROBABLY HAS TO CHARGE OR SOMETHING.
I SHOULD HEAD HOME.
ME TOO.

THE NEXT MORNING . . .
MOM! YOU DON'T . . .
. . . USUALLY HAVE YOUR COFFEE IN MY ROOM.
WHAT'S UP?
SEEMS THERE WAS SOME SORT OF INCIDENT AT THE MALL YESTERDAY AFTERNOON.
THE EMPORIUM HAD TO CALL SECURITY AND EVERYTHING.
ALL OVER SOME STUPID TOY. APPARENTLY, A COUPLE OF KIDS EVEN MADE OFF WITH ONE DURING THE COMMOTION.
CAN YOU BELIEVE THAT?

MUST'VE BEEN AFTER WE GOT THERE.
YEAH, YOU'VE GOTTA GO.

THAT AFTERNOON . . .
LISTEN . . . FIRST-GENERATION TECHNOLOGY IS ALWAYS BOGUS. WE'LL SAVE UP FOR GEN TWO, GIVE THEM A CHANCE TO WORK OUT THE BUGS.
THANKS, RAJ . . .
WHAT HAPPENS IF WE SEE THOSE SECURITY GUARDS AGAIN?
WHAT ARE THEY GOING TO DO? ARREST US FOR RETURNING WHAT WE STOLE?
GOOD POINT.
HAL'S HALLOWEEN HALL WAY
DRESS
WAIT. . . WHAT?
DID WE COME IN THE WRONG ENTRANCE?

DID WE FALL THROUGH A WORMHOLE OR SOMETHING?
WHERE'S THE EMPORIUM?
THE WHAT?
THE STORE THAT WAS HERE BEFORE. WHERE'D IT GO?
NOT A CLUE. I JUST STARTED TODAY.
BUT I NEED TO RETURN THIS.
IS THAT WHAT I THINK IT IS? WHY WOULD YOU WANT TO RETURN IT? YOU COULD SELL THAT THING FOR A FORTUNE.
IT'S . . . IT'S NOT MINE.
IT IS NOW.
WE'RE GOING FOR A KIND OF MURDEROUS FAIRY VIBE.
I CAN'T RETURN IT.
WELL . . . NO ONE CAN SAY WE DIDN'T TRY.
MAYBE IT'S FOR THE BEST . . .

THAT NIGHT . . .
THIS YEAR, WE'RE GONNA WIN HALLOWEEN.
EVERY YEAR, WE VOW TO MAKE IT TO THE OTHER SIDE OF THE TRAIN TRACKS, WHERE ALL THE GOOD CANDY IS.
AND EVERY YEAR, WE RUN OUT OF TIME, DISTRACTED BY THE FALSE PROMISE OF THE GOOD STUFF IN OUR OWN NEIGHBORHOOD.
DO NOT PARK
NOT THIS YEAR. THIS YEAR WE START ON THE OTHER SIDE OF THE TRACKS AND WORK OUR WAY BACK.
THAT STORM'S GETTING SERIOUS . . .
AND SO IS MY WINNING STREAK!
COME ON! POWER OUTAGES WARRANT A REDO!

WHY ARE YOU STILL MESSING WITH THAT?
PRESS ANY BUTTON
HM?
HE'S RIGHT. IT'S HOPELESS, OSCAR. JUST LET IT GO.
LITERALLY. AS IN GET RID OF IT. IT'S NOT JUST BROKEN. IT'S . . .
. . . WRONG.
I DON'T KNOW. WE GOT AWAY FROM MALL SECURITY. I KEPT THE TRUTH FROM MY MOM. WE CAN'T RETURN IT. THERE HAS TO BE SOME REASON. I WANT TO SEE IT WORK.
A PORT . . .
RIIIIIING
I'LL GET IT.
YEAH, DUDE. IT'S YOUR HOUSE.

HELLO?
HELLO? CAN YOU HEAR ME?
HELLO? HELLO, OSCAR ARE YOU THERE?
UGH, THIS STORM. YES. CAN YOU HEAR ME? IT'S MOM.
I CAN HEAR YOU.
LITTLE MAN, I NEED YOUR HELP TOMORROW.
SURE, MOM.
I'M SORRY TO ASK. YOU KNOW HOW MUCH I HATE ASKING. IT'S JUST THAT WITH THIS STORM TONIGHT, WE'VE HAD SO MANY PEOPLE CALL IN SICK, WE'RE GOING TO BE COMPLETELY BACKED UP ON LAUNDRY AND CHARTS TOMORROW, AND . . .
. . . ARE YOU LISTENING?
UH-HUH . . .
WAIT, NO, MOM. NO, NOT TOMORROW.
I KNEW YOU'D BE UPSET, HON, BUT IT'S-
MOM, TOMORROW IS HALLOWEEN!
I REALIZE THAT, BUT SWEETIE, AREN'T YOU AND YOUR FRIENDS A LITTLE OLD TO BE . . .
NO! WHY DO YOU ALWAYS DO THAT?
DO WHAT?
YOU ACT LIKE I'M OLDER. YOU NEVER LET ME BE A KID.
DAD DIED, AND YOU EXPECTED ME TO JUST GROW UP.

OSCAR, I-
I STOLE IT, OKAY? I STOLE THE STUPID PLUSHTRAP TOY. YOUR LITTLE MAN STOLE IT!
B-BOOM
MOM?
BEEEEEEEEEP

RAJ, I NEED YOUR CELL PHONE CHARGER.
WHAT? RIGHT NOW? I WAS JUST CATCHING UP!
NO, YOU WEREN'T.
FRONT POUCH OF MY BACKPACK. GET IT YOURSELF.
THIS IS IT, RAJ. I'M PUTTING YOU OUT OF YOUR MISERY IN . . .
THREE . . .
IT FITS!
TWO . . .
ONE . . .

FZZTTBOOOOOM
THUNK
OSCAR!
OSCAR!
OSCAR, HOW MANY FINGERS AM I HOLDING UP?
YOU'RE NOT HOLDING ANYTHING UP.
RIGHT. SORRY. ARE YOU OKAY?
I'M FINE.
I THINK YOU WERE HIT BY LIGHTNING, DUDE.
MAYBE WE SHOULD CALL HIS MOM.
OKAY, NOW I KNOW HE'S FINE.
NO! NO, DON'T CALL HER.

YEAH, IT'S DEAD.
IT'S NOT YOUR FAULT. IT LOOKS LIKE ELECTRICITY IS OUT ACROSS THIS WHOLE END OF TOWN.
OF COURSE EVERYTHING IS STILL FINE ON THE OTHER SIDE OF THE TRACKS . . .
WE'LL JUST HAVE TO MAKE OUR WAY TO THE SLEEPING BAGS, AND GET SICK ON SCORCHING HOT CHEESE KNOBS AND KNOCK OUT TOMORROW NIGHT'S TRICK-OR-TREATING ROUTE ON MY PHONE.
GREAT . . .
SOMETHING ELSE TO APOLOGIZE FOR.
I BLAME YOU.

LIGHT'S OUT.
WHAT DID YOU SAY?
HUH?
YOU HEARD THAT, RIGHT?
HEARD WHAT?
NEVER MIND . . .
STORM'S MAKING ME HEAR THINGS . . .

WE START SOUTH, THEN WORK OUR WAY NORTH.
BUT WE'LL WASTE ALL OUR TIME IN TRANSIT. WHAT ABOUT MOVING FASTER BETWEEN HOUSES IF WE'RE NOT ALREADY WEIGHED DOWN BY CANDY? AERODYNAMICS.
WELL, WE NEED TO PICK SOON, BECAUSE MY PHONE'S NEARLY DEAD.
OSCAR, YOU BREAK THE TIE. WHERE DO WE START? NORTH OR SOUTH END OF THE TRACKS?
I CAN'T GO.
IT'S MY MOM. SHE NEEDS . . .
NOOO!
EH . . . CHILL OUT, RAJ. IT'LL BE LAME ANYWAY.
YEAH, UH . . . YOU'RE RIGHT. I BET THE FULL-SIZE CANDY BARS ARE JUST A MYTH.
AND WE'LL SPLIT THE STASH THREE WAYS.
THANKS, GUYS . . .
WHOA, IS THAT A WHITE STREAK IN YOUR HAIR?

SERIOUSLY?
HA HA, NO, BUT I'M SURE YOU FRIED A FEW BRAIN CELLS BACK THERE.
HA HA . . .
AW . . . THERE GOES THE PHONE. I NEVER SHOULD HAVE LET YOU USE MY CHARGER.
WOULDN'T HAVE DONE MUCH GOOD WITH NO ELECTRICITY IN THIS ENTIRE HALF OF TOWN.
OH YEAH-
THUNK
WHAT WAS THAT?
DID YOU GET A CAT OR SOMETHING?

THUMP
MAYBE A TREE BRANCH AGAINST THE WINDOW.
THIS IS STUPID.
THUMP
HANG ON . . .
THUNK
SCCCRRRTT... SCRTCCTHHHH... CRUNCH...
SO IT WAS A "NO" ON THE CAT, THEN.
AND I DON'T THINK A TREE CLIMBED INTO MY ROOM, EITHER.
YOU GUYS, SHUT UP!

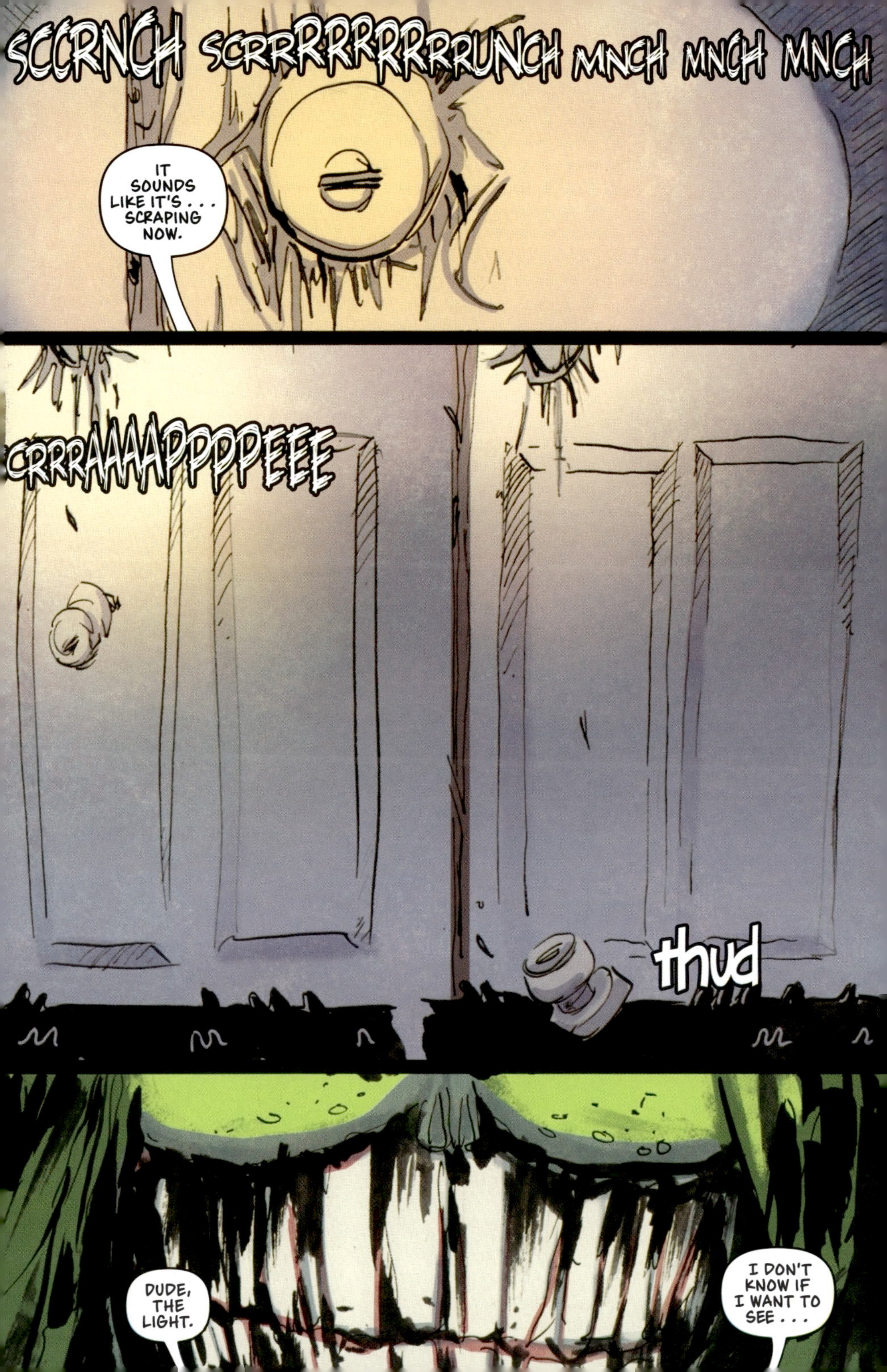

SCCRNCH SCRRRRRRRRRRUNCH MNCH MNCH MNCH

IT SOUNDS LIKE IT'S . . . SCRAPING NOW.

CRRRAAAAPPPPPEEE

thud

NO WAY . . .
I THOUGHT IT WAS BROKEN!
CAN WE PLEASE ARGUE ABOUT THIS SOMEWHERE ELSE?
DUDE, IT'S A TOY. WHAT DO YOU THINK IT'S GONNA-

AAAAAH!
GO GO GO!

CRAK

IN HERE!

SLAM
TCHKT

BANG
SKKKRRTCHH . . .
CRUNCH
HOW DO WE STOP THIS THING? THE SWITCH IS UNDER ITS FOOT, RIGHT?
QUICK, CLIMB UP ON SOMETHING. THE HIGHEST THING YOU CAN!

thud

CRUNCH MNCH
SCRKKKTTCHHHH
CRNTCH CRNTCH

ARE YOU KIDDING ME?!

THINK OF SOMETHING! SOMEBODY THINK OF SOMETHING FAST!
HOW DO WE TURN IT OFF?!
THE LIGHT!
THE BOX SAID IT FREEZES IN THE LIGHT!
IT STOPPED . . .
IT CAN'T MOVE AS LONG AS OSCAR KEEPS THE LIGHT ON IT . . .
EASY FOR YOU TO SAY. KEEP IT STEADY . . .
OVER HERE!

RAJ? HOW'D YOU GET OVER-
PUT IT BACK! PUT IT BACK!!!
SORRY! SORRY!

CUTE TRICK, THROWING YOUR VOICE, RAJ. THINK MAYBE YOU COULD PRACTICE YOUR VENTRILOQUIST ACT SOME OTHER TIME?
IT CAN MIMIC OUR VOICES, TO DISTRACT US . . .
I DON'T THINK THAT WAS ACTUALLY RAJ . . .
SERIOUSLY???
WE GOTTA GET OUT OF HERE.
LEAVE THE FLASHLIGHT HERE, RIGHT ON IT. WE BARRICADE THE DOOR AND CALL FOR–
HOW?

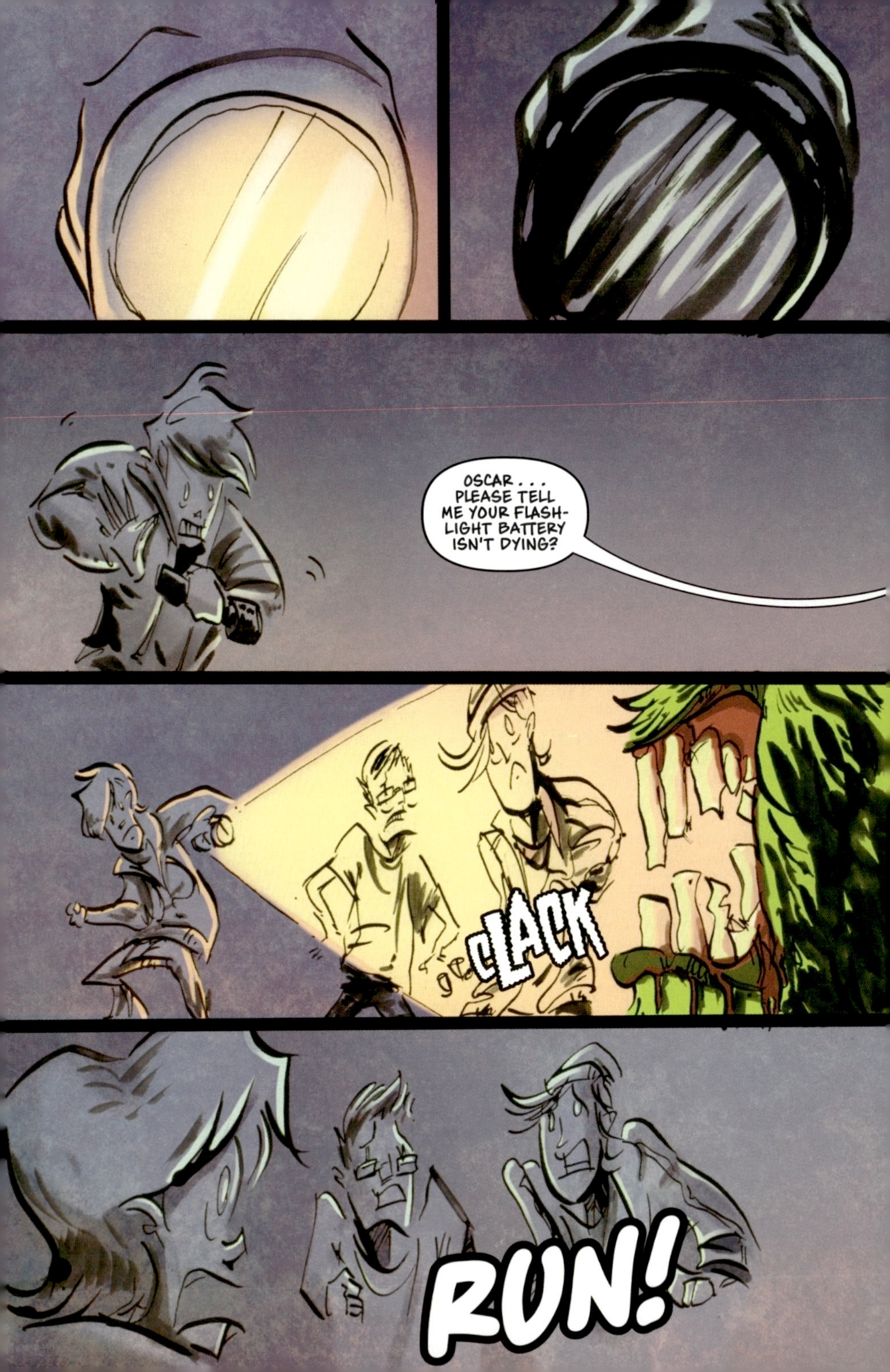

OSCAR . . .
PLEASE TELL
ME YOUR FLASH-
LIGHT BATTERY
ISN'T DYING?

SLAM
BACK TO SQUARE ONE! HOW DO WE KEEP THAT FROM HAPPENING AGAIN?!
HERE'S WHAT WE DO. I'LL KEEP THE LIGHT AIMED ON THE DOOR. YOU TWO OPEN IT. THE LIGHT WILL HIT THE PLUSHTRAP AND IT'LL FREEZE.
WE ALL GET OUT, THEN KEEP THE LIGHT ON IT AS WE LEAVE THE HOUSE.
BAD IDEA . . . HORRIBLE IDEA . . .
BUT . . . OUR ONLY IDEA.
READY?

GET IT! GET IT GET IT GET IT!
YOU SURE ABOUT THIS?
NOPE. JUST HURRY.

HANG ON, OSCAR. HOW ARE YOU GOING TO GET PAST? THE LIGHT HAS TO BE IN ITS EYES FOR IT TO FREEZE.
YEAH, SORRY, BUDDY. I NEED YOU TO HOLD THE LIGHT OVER ITS HEAD, BETWEEN ITS EARS . . .
AW, MAN . . .
WHY DID I ASK?
JUST KEEP IT STEADY, PLEASE . . .
ONCE I'M OUT . . . WE BACK DOWN THE HALL, AND . . .

LITTLE MAN, I NEED YOUR HELP!
MS. AVILA! STAY THERE, DON'T MOVE!
ISAAC, THE LIGHT!
SORRY!

ISAAC, THE FLASHLIGHT . . .
I MUST HAVE SHAKEN THE BATTERY LOOSE OR SOMETHING!
RUUUUN!!!!

SKKKRTCH... SKRTCH SKRTCH
WE MADE IT...
FOR NOW.
I DON'T THINK EVEN YOUR FRONT DOOR IS GOING TO HOLD IT FOR THAT MUCH LONGER.

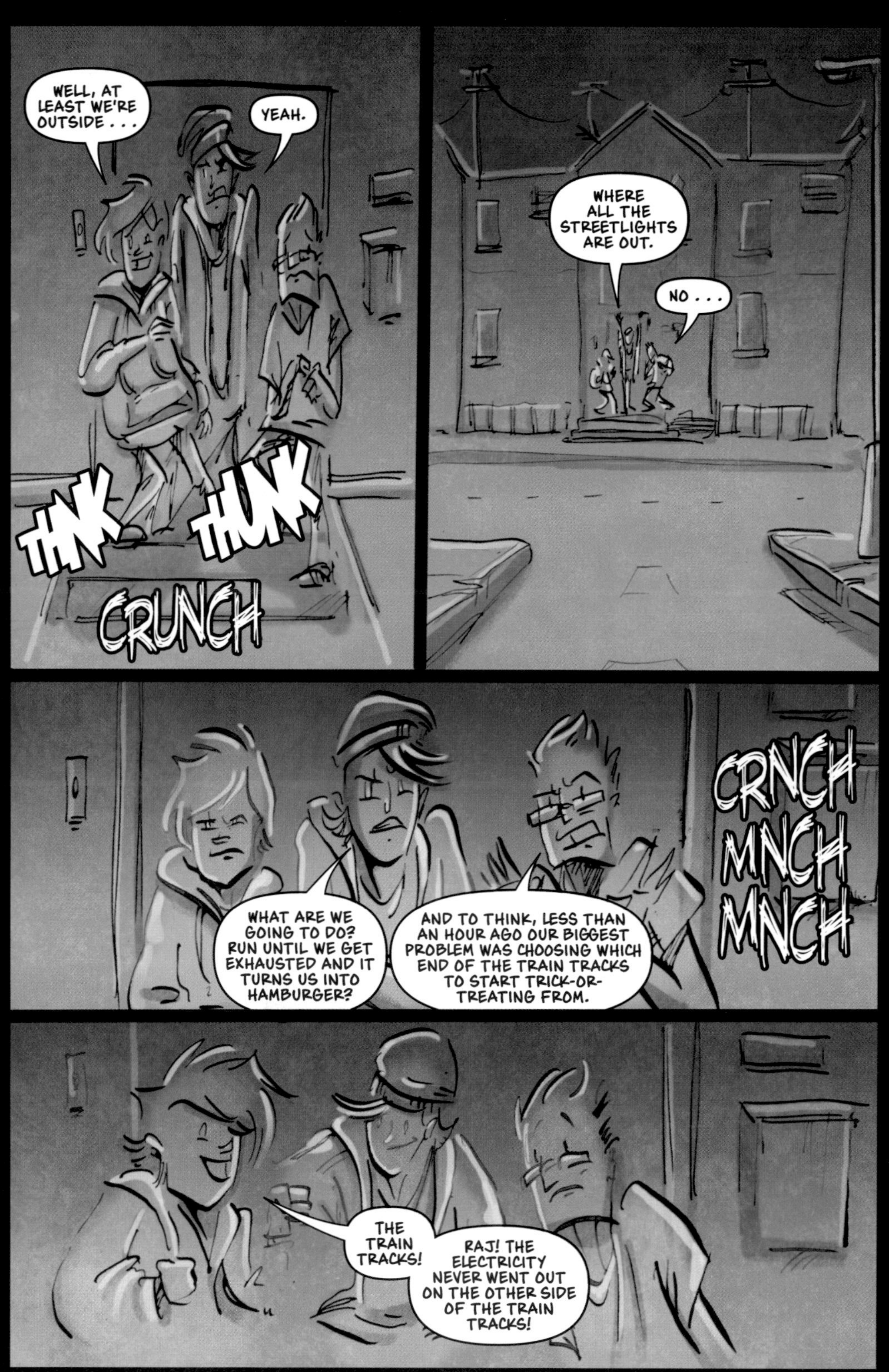
WELL, AT LEAST WE'RE OUTSIDE . . .
YEAH.
THNK
THUNK
CRUNCH
WHERE ALL THE STREETLIGHTS ARE OUT.
NO . . .
CRNCH
MNCH
MNCH
WHAT ARE WE GOING TO DO? RUN UNTIL WE GET EXHAUSTED AND IT TURNS US INTO HAMBURGER?
AND TO THINK, LESS THAN AN HOUR AGO OUR BIGGEST PROBLEM WAS CHOOSING WHICH END OF THE TRAIN TRACKS TO START TRICK-OR-TREATING FROM.
THE TRAIN TRACKS!
RAJ! THE ELECTRICITY NEVER WENT OUT ON THE OTHER SIDE OF THE TRAIN TRACKS!

FOLLOW ME!
WHAM
IT'S NOT STOPPING . . .

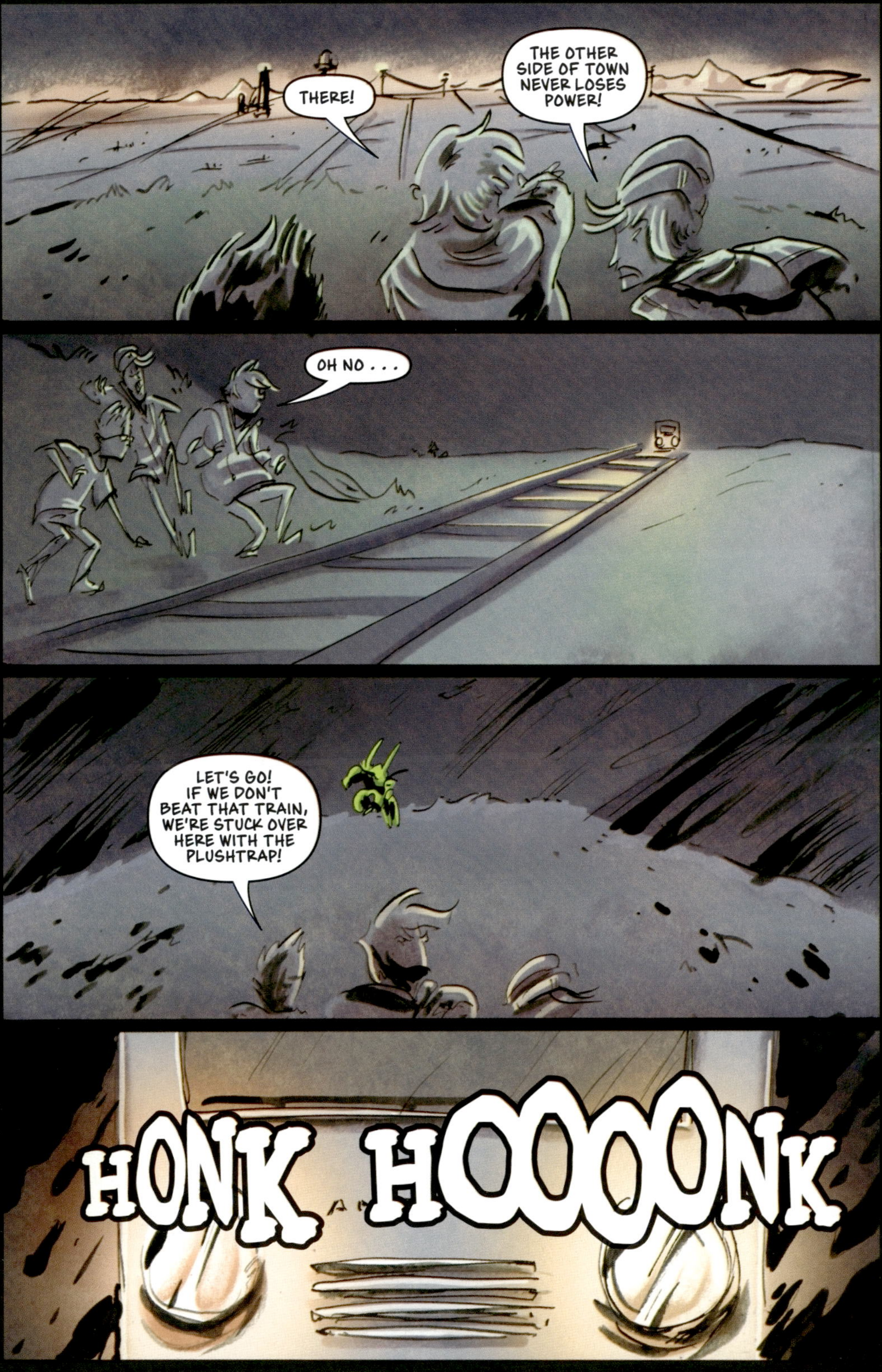

THERE!

THE OTHER SIDE OF TOWN NEVER LOSES POWER!

OH NO . . .

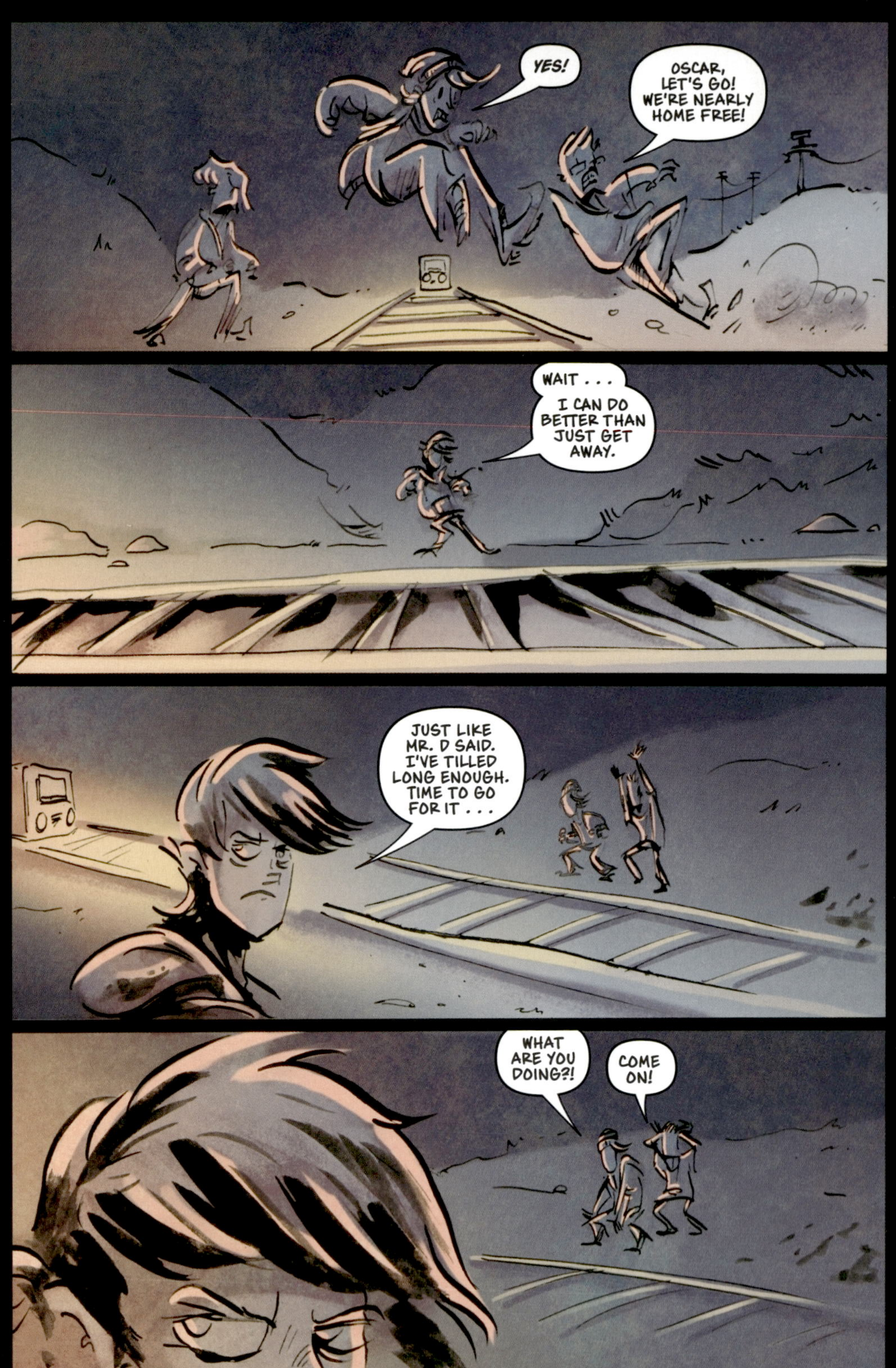
YES!
OSCAR, LET'S GO! WE'RE NEARLY HOME FREE!
WAIT . . .
I CAN DO BETTER THAN JUST GET AWAY.
JUST LIKE MR. D SAID. I'VE TILLED LONG ENOUGH. TIME TO GO FOR IT . . .
WHAT ARE YOU DOING?!
COME ON!

AMTRA
LITTLE MAN, I NEED YOU!

C-CRASH-A-SLAM
HOOOOOOOOOONNNNNKKK
DID . . .
DID I DIE?
HONESTLY, I DON'T KNOW HOW, BUT NO.
YOU'RE AN IDIOT.
I KNOW.

HA HA . . .
HA HA HA . . .
HA HA HA HA HA!
LET'S GO HOME.

HALLOWEEN . . .
KNOCK KNOCK
REVERSE TRICK-OR-TREAT!
WANT SOME CANDY, MR. D?
I SEE MARILYN'S FEELING BOLD.
DARN RIGHT, I DO! COME ON IN, OSCAR.
I DECIDED THAT IF SHE'S GOING TO STEAL MY SOUL, SHE'S EARNED THE RIGHT.
SO LONG AS YOU TWO ARE GETTING ALONG.
HOW'D YOUR HARVEST GO?
BAD CROP THIS YEAR.
BUT I'M GLAD I DID THE DIGGING.

BREAK
I GOT YOU SOME OF THOSE CHOCOLATE-COVERED ALMONDS YOU LIKE.
I STILL HAD SOME MONEY LEFT OVER AFTER THE WHOLE . . .
. . . TOY THING.

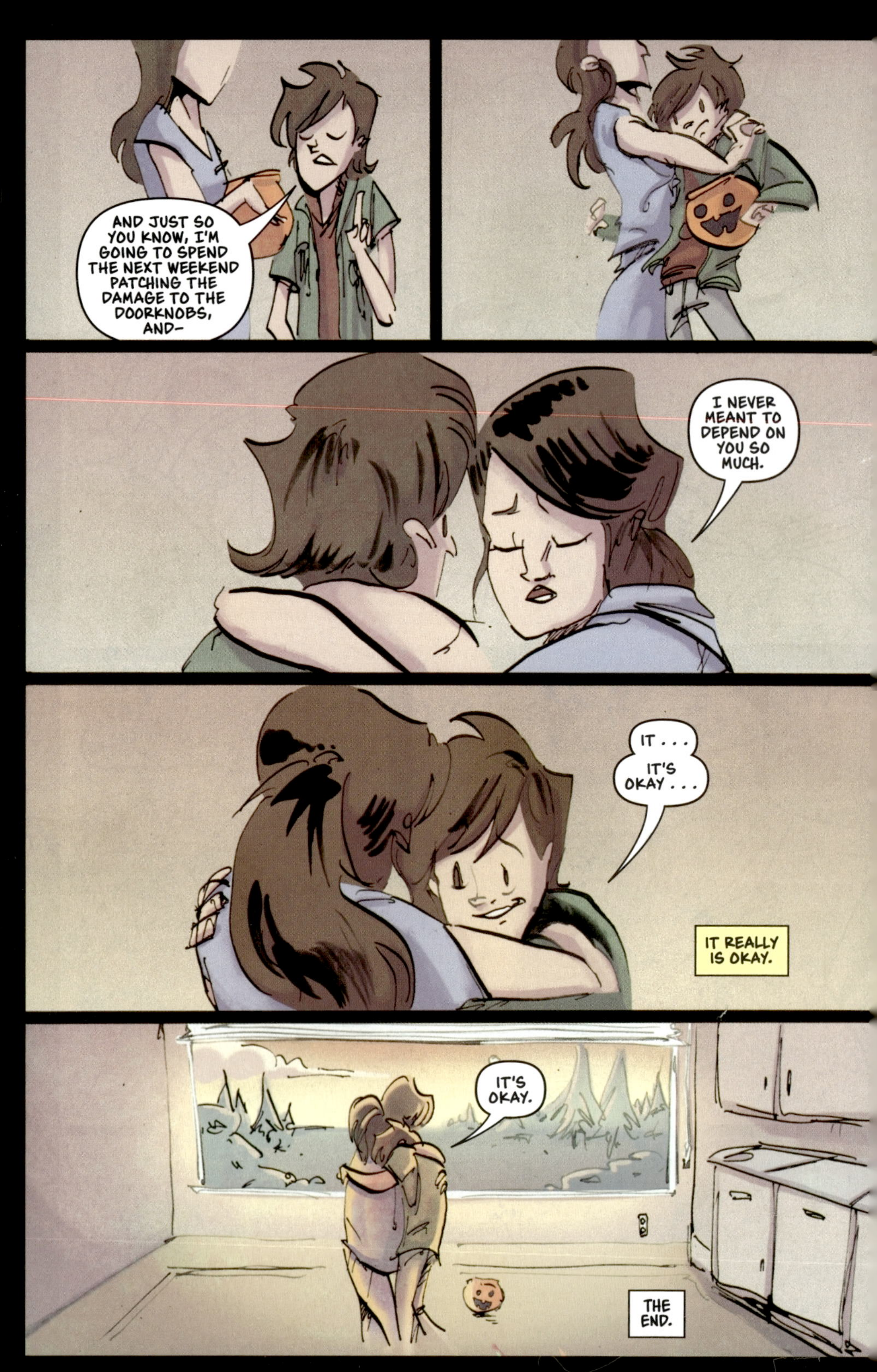

AND JUST SO YOU KNOW, I'M GOING TO SPEND THE NEXT WEEKEND PATCHING THE DAMAGE TO THE DOORKNOBS, AND–
I NEVER MEANT TO DEPEND ON YOU SO MUCH.
IT . . .
IT'S OKAY . . .
IT REALLY IS OKAY.
IT'S OKAY.
THE END.